February 2008

THE OPPOSABLE MIND

THE
OPPOSABLE
MIND

How Successful Leaders
Win Through Integrative Thinking

Roger L. Martin

HARVARD BUSINESS SCHOOL PRESS

BOSTON, MASSACHUSETTS

Library of Congress Cataloging-in-Publication Data

Martin, Roger L.
  The opposable mind : how successful leaders win through integrative
thinking / Roger L. Martin.
    p. cm.
  ISBN-13: 978-1-4221-1892-4 (hardcover : alk. paper)
  1. Leadership—Psychological aspects. 2. Thought and thinking.
3. Contradiction. 4. Problem solving. 5. Decision making. 6. Successful
people—Interviews. I. Title.
  HD57.7.M39248 2007
  658.4'092—dc22

                                                    2007021447

This book is dedicated to

Marcel Desautels,

integrative thinking visionary.

Contents

Acknowledgments

I HAVE MANY FRIENDS AND COLLEAGUES to thank for essential help on this book. First and foremost, I owe a huge intellectual debt of gratitude to my two closest thinking partners, Hilary Austen Johnson and Mihnea Moldoveanu, without whom I would not have been able to write this book.

I met Hilary in 1995 during the research for her dissertation at Stanford University (Hilary Austen Johnson, "Artistry in Practice," 1998, available in the Stanford University Library) under James March and Elliot Eisner. She introduced me to March's work in organizational learning and Eisner's in qualitative research, both of which played instrumental roles in the development of the book. Hilary's dissertation explored how a person develops artistic knowledge, and her framework underpins the entire second half of this book. In addition, my interview technique for the leaders in the book was influenced by the technique she developed for her dissertation. Finally, the first rudimentary idea behind the model in the first half of the book was sketched out on Hilary's porch in Santa Cruz, California, in 2001. I strongly recommend reading Hilary's recent article on artistry (Hilary Austen Johnson, "Artistry for the Strategist," *Journal of Business Strategy* [volume 28, issue 4, 2007: 13–21]).

I met Mihnea when he joined the faculty of the Rotman School in the summer of 1999, one year after I came to Rotman as dean, and he has been my primary thinking partner in the faculty ever since. In 2002, he became the academic director of the Desautels Centre for Integrative Thinking, which leads all of our integrative thinking research and teaching. He has introduced me to analytic philosophy and history of science, which has had a profound influence on my thinking. As perhaps the best-read person I know, Mihnea has the ability to connect my thinking to scholarly work I would have otherwise had no chance to discover, such as the writings of American fallibilist philosopher Charles Sanders Peirce, whose thinking features prominently in chapter 6. He has also been instrumental in developing the integrative thinking teaching program at the Rotman School that has enabled us to put our research work into action.

A core group of fellow travelers at the school has been nursing along the integrative thinking agenda and has provided continuous support on the development of the ideas in the book. Suzanne Spragge coteaches all of my integrative thinking courses and has supported the development of the thinking in the book. Jennifer Riel has been my research associate for the book. And Melanie Carr, who is a psychiatrist by training, has helped me think about the emotional challenges to building integrative thinking capacity.

Before I started writing the book in the summer of 2006, Malcolm Gladwell convened a talented group of writers and editors to give me advice. Writers Gladwell (*Tipping Point* and *Blink*) and James Surowiecki (*The Wisdom of Crowds*) and editors Henry Finder (*New Yorker*) and Bruce Headlam (*New York Times*) provided invaluable advice on structuring the book, and Bruce came up with the idea that became the eventual title (thank you, Bruce!). Malcolm and Bruce provided valuable follow-up feedback on manuscripts.

A dozen colleagues and friends read the manuscript for me and provided valuable written feedback for which I am hugely grateful. I sincerely thank Joel Baum, Brendan Calder, Petra Cooper, Nancy Lockhart, Terry Martin, Bob McDonald, Sally Osberg, Joe Rotman, David Smith, Lynn Utter, Larry Wasser, and Craig Wynett. My mentor, Rob Prichard, former president of the University of Toronto, gave me important advice on how to better utilize my huge stock of successful leader interviews, and for that I am grateful. A former student, Dave Eden, introduced me to a century-old *Science* article by Thomas Chamberlin that figured more prominently in the book than Dave ever imagined, I suspect.

My Rotman colleague Steve Arenburg was instrumental in organizing the visits of all the successful leaders to Rotman School. Though they are among the busiest men and women in the world, they all came away feeling that Steve had made their visits a pleasure and time well spent. Bob Fleck of Teamwork Communications expertly filmed the discussions to capture them for posterity. Karen Christensen, our brilliant *Rotman Magazine* editor, has helped me develop ways to describe integrative thinking in articles in the magazine since 1999.

I took a leave of absence during the summer of 2006 to focus on writing the first full manuscript of the book. I couldn't have done so without hurting the progress of the Rotman School, had it not been for the presence of the school's two fantastic vice deans, Jim Fisher and Peter Pauly, and CAO Mary-Ellen Yeomans, who ran the school in my place for the summer. I was slightly chagrined to find that I wasn't missed at all!

Jeff Kehoe, senior editor at Harvard Business School Press, and I had long talks before starting this book project and he encouraged me to bring this proposal to him. He has been a great publishing partner and has brought to bear the terrific team at HBSP to support the book.

When I turned to finding an editor to help me transform the initial manuscript into a final book, I thought back to my most pleasant collaborations with Harris Collingwood, who was the senior editor at *Harvard Business Review* who worked with me on my article, "The Virtue Matrix: Calculating the Return on Corporate Responsibility" (*Harvard Business Review*, March 2002). Harris has made wonderful improvements to everything about the book. Readers can be thankful that Harris makes words disappear without being missed! Someday, I would like to be able to write as well as him.

Last, but certainly not least, I thank my magnificent agent Tina Bennett. Tina represents everything an author would ever want in an agent. When she believes a book should be written, she will let nothing stand in the way of its publication. She supported this project from its inception and made sure it ended up at the right publisher with the requisite amount of attention. She was calm but determined throughout, regardless of how agitated I happened to be at the time. She is a true friend to whom I owe much of my publishing career to date.

I hope that you enjoy this book, and more importantly, that it helps you make the most of your personal potential for greatness. All the people mentioned above have contributed to that possibility, but only you can take the requisite actions. I hope that *The Opposable Mind* will motivate you to do so; if it does, I will have fulfilled a labor of love.

1

Choices, Conflict, and the Creative Spark

The Problem-Solving Power of Integrative Thinking

The test of a first-rate intelligence is the ability to hold two opposing ideas in mind at the same time and still retain the ability to function. One should, for example, be able to see that things are hopeless yet be determined to make them otherwise.[1]

—F. Scott Fitzgerald

IT WAS SEPTEMBER 1999, and Michael Lee-Chin had a serious crisis on his hands—the worst crisis of his business career. Lee-Chin had presided over more than ten years of remarkable growth at his beloved money management firm, AIC Limited, but now AIC was under withering attack. Its very survival was in doubt. Things did indeed look hopeless, but Lee-Chin was absolutely determined to make them otherwise.

1

Integrative Thinking and the Rescue of AIC

Lee-Chin had seen hard times before. The eldest of nine children of biracial parents (both parents were the offspring of Jamaican mothers and Chinese fathers); Lee-Chin was something of an outcast in his hometown of Port Antonio, Jamaica. Other children in the neighborhood teased Michael and his siblings, and he felt, he told me, "betwixt and between," neither fully Chinese nor fully Jamaican.[2]

Proud and entrepreneurial, Michael's mother and stepfather worked as clerks at the local market, and his mother took on second and third jobs as a bookkeeper and an Avon lady. With the money they managed to save, his parents eventually opened their own market, but money and luxuries were still scarce, and it was inconceivable that their oldest child would one day earn a spot on the *Forbes* global list of billionaires.[3]

In 1970, Lee-Chin moved to Canada, where he attended Mc-Master University in Hamilton, Ontario. After graduating, he worked odd jobs, including road engineer and bar bouncer, while he looked for his true calling. With his warm, friendly manner, quick wit, and room-filling presence—he's six feet, four inches tall—Michael was a natural salesman, and he discovered in himself a passion for investing. In 1983, he borrowed $400,000 to put to work in the stock market, and by 1987 he had earned enough to buy AIC Limited, a tiny investment advisory firm managing a mere $600,000 in investors' assets.[4]

An admirer of Warren Buffett, Lee-Chin pursued a strategy at AIC with almost no parallel in the mutual fund business. The typical mutual fund manager holds one hundred to two hundred different stocks at any given time and turns over the entire portfolio every eighteen months or so. But emulating Buffett's approach of taking long-term stakes in a relative handful of companies, Lee-Chin's AIC Advantage Fund would hold ten to twenty stocks and hang onto them, as he says, "more or less forever." Lee-Chin's "buy, hold, and prosper" philosophy worked brilliantly, and by 1999, assets under management had grown 10,000-fold, to $6 billion.

But in 1999, as we heard so often at the time, everything was different. Investors were clamoring to buy Internet service providers, dot-coms, and switching-gear start-ups, day-trading was suddenly respectable, and a mutual fund with a buy and hold philosophy and a portfolio of financial, manufacturing, and grocery store stocks seemed hopelessly old-fashioned and out of step. Many investors lost faith in AIC's investing approach, and for the first time in its history, the Advantage Fund was suffering substantial net redemptions—more money was flowing out of the fund than new money was flowing in.

The low point for AIC and Lee-Chin arrived on the morning of September 2, 1999. Lee-Chin opened his newspaper that day to find that one of the most influential business columnists in Canada was trashing AIC's basic business model and calling on investors to get out while their holdings were still worth something. The article predicted that to raise enough cash to meet the tide of redemptions, AIC would have to sell many of the Advantage Fund holdings. The columnist speculated that the forced asset sales would further depress the price of the stocks held in the fund, which in turn would drive down its returns still further, prompting even more redemptions.

The new redemptions would require more stock sales, reinforcing a downward spiral that would continue until there was, for all intents and purposes, no more AIC.[5]

Lee-Chin remembers that morning well. "I felt awful!" he admitted to me. But despite his distress, he sensed that an opportunity lurked within the crisis that engulfed AIC. The Chinese character for "crisis," he pointed out to me, combines the characters for "danger" and "opportunity."

Lee-Chin had to choose, and quickly. Would he sell shares to cover the redemptions, concede that his "buy, hold, and prosper" strategy was fatally flawed, and diversify into the technology stocks that were the flavor of the month? That might save the firm, but at the price of everything he believed in and valued as an investor. Or would he stick to his principles, hold his ground, and risk the firm's falling into a death spiral that might destroy the business he had built nearly from scratch?

He collected himself, thought hard—but not long—and made his choice. The option he selected was . . . neither. Or rather, both. "The marketplace was expecting that we had to sell," he told me. "I said, 'What if we didn't sell? What if we turned around and bought? Then what?' We'd turn the assumptions upside down and upset the whole applecart."

Lee-Chin had little choice but to sell some of the Advantage Fund's holdings to meet redemptions. But then he took a startling tack. The marketplace expected AIC to use any money left over after meeting redemptions to load up on technology stocks. Lee-Chin would confound those expectations. "Okay," he decided, "we're going to identify this one stock, Mackenzie Financial Corporation. We're just going to put everything we have into purchasing that one stock." He poured every cent he could pry from AIC's corporate coffers, and every dollar he could raise from banks, into Mackenzie, one of the fund's major holdings and a stock he and his staff knew well. "We did everything to buy Mackenzie," he recalled. "The share price went from $15 to $18 overnight. The rest is history. Mackenzie was sold [in April 2001] for $30 per share. Our unit holders made $400 million, and we made a handsome return."

His move didn't just save AIC. It helped AIC become Canada's largest privately held mutual fund company, in the process making Lee-Chin a billionaire. His wealth has provided him with the wherewithal to buy and turn around the National Commercial Bank Jamaica, Jamaica's largest bank, and fund philanthropic projects in Jamaica, Canada, and beyond.

The Integrative Thinker's Advantage

The lessons of AIC's cash crisis, and Lee-Chin's response to it, may seem to have limited application to other business dilemmas. But Lee-Chin's bold counterattack wasn't just a spur-of-the-moment gamble by a swashbuckling Jamaican entrepreneur, in response to an unrepeatable set of circumstances. The thinking process Lee-Chin followed is, I believe, common to some of the most innovative and successful people in the business world today, whatever their domain or the problems they encounter.

I have spent the past fifteen years, first as a management consultant and then as the dean of a business school, studying leaders who have striking and exemplary success records, trying to discern a shared theme running through their successes. Over the past six years, I have interviewed more than fifty such leaders—

some for as long as eight hours—and as I listened, a common theme has emerged with striking clarity. The leaders I have studied share at least one trait, aside from their talent for innovation and long-term business success. They have the predisposition and the capacity to hold two diametrically opposing ideas in their heads. And then, without panicking or simply settling for one alternative or the other, they're able to produce a synthesis that is superior to either opposing idea. *Integrative thinking* is my term for this process—or more precisely this discipline of consideration and synthesis—that is the hallmark of exceptional businesses and the people who run them.

As I listened to some of the sharpest minds in business talk about how they thought through the most pressing and perplexing dilemmas of their careers, I searched for a metaphor that could give me deeper insight into the dynamic of their thinking. The skill with which these thinkers held two opposing ideas in fruitful tension reminded me of the way other highly skilled people use their hands. Human beings, it's well known, are distinguished from nearly every other creature by a physical feature known as the opposable thumb. Thanks to the tension we can create by opposing the thumb and fingers, we can do marvelous things that no other creature can do—write, thread a needle, carve a diamond, paint a picture, guide a catheter up through an artery to unblock it. All those actions would be impossible without the crucial tension between the thumb and fingers.

Evolution provided human beings with a valuable potential advantage. But that potential would have gone to waste if our species had not exploited it by using it in ever more sophisticated ways. When we set out to learn to write or to sew, paint, or golf, we practice using our opposable thumbs, training both the key muscles involved and the brain that controls them. Without exploring the possibilities of opposition, we wouldn't have developed either its physical properties or the cognition that accompanies and animates it.

Similarly, we were born with an *opposable mind* we can use to hold two conflicting ideas in constructive tension. We can use that tension to think our way through to a new and superior idea. Were we able to hold only one thought or idea in our heads at a time, we wouldn't have access to the insights that the opposable mind can produce. And just as we can develop and refine the skill with which we employ our opposable thumbs to perform tasks that once seemed impossible, I'm convinced we can also, with patient practice, develop the ability to use our opposable minds to unlock solutions to problems that seem to resist every effort to solve them. I won't go so far as to say that every problem will find a resolution as brilliantly elegant and successful as the one that Lee-Chin arrived at. But in our daily lives, we often face problems that appear to admit of two equally unsatisfactory solutions. Using our opposable minds to move past unappetizing alternatives, we can find solutions that once appeared beyond the reach of our imaginations.

I'm hardly the first to notice this remarkable capacity of the human mind. Sixty years ago, F. Scott Fitzgerald saw "the ability to hold two opposing ideas in mind at the same time and still retain the ability to function" as the sign of "a first-rate intelligence." That last phrase is telling. In Fitzgerald's view, only people who have the highest levels of native intelligence have the capacity to use their opposable minds to create new models.

Fitzgerald, I think, is too quick to suggest that the opposable mind is exclusive to geniuses. It's true that all the people I hold up as examples in this book possess first-rate intelligence, and, just as crucially, the temperaments to put opposing ideas into play without being paralyzed by fear and anxiety. But my view is closer to that of another student of the opposable mind, Thomas C. Chamberlin. A scholar (he was president of the University of Wisconsin from 1887 to 1892) and naturalist, Chamberlin in 1890 proposed the idea of "multiple working hypotheses" as an improvement over the most commonly employed scientific method of the time, the "working hypothesis," by which the scientist tests the validity of a single explanatory concept through trial and error and experimentation. In an article published in *Science*—then as now one of the world's most prestigious peer-reviewed scientific journals—Chamberlin wrote:

> *In following a single hypothesis, the mind is presumably led to a single explanatory conception. But an adequate explanation often involves the co-ordination of several agencies, which enter into the combined result in varying proportions. The true explanation is therefore necessarily complex. Such complex explanations of phenomena are specially encouraged by the method of multiple hypotheses, and constitute one of its chief merits.*[6]

Interviews with more than fifty great managerial leaders have led me to concur with Chamberlin and Fitzgerald: thinkers who exploit opposing ideas to construct a new solution enjoy a built-in advantage over thinkers who can consider only one model at a time.

The ability to use the opposable mind is an advantage at any time, in any era. But the opposable mind may be more than an advantage in today's world. In this information-saturated age, where each new bit of data complicates a picture that is already staggeringly complex, integrative thinking may be a necessity if we are ever to find our way past the multiple binds in which we find ourselves. Certainly the business world seems ripe for a new approach to problem solving.

In business, we often look at decisions as a series of either-or propositions, of trade-offs. We can either have steady growth or we can pioneer adventurous new ways of designing, building, and selling things. We can either keep costs down, or we can invest in better stores and service. Either we can serve our shareholders, or we can serve our communities. But what if there was a way to satisfy both customers and shareholders without sacrificing the needs and interests of either party? What if we could find a way to meet demands for growth and still be a responsible steward of the environment? To pursue innovation while maintaining the continuity that large organizations need to function effectively?

Integrative thinking shows us a way past the binary limits of either–or. It shows us that there's a way to integrate the advantages of one solution without canceling out the advantages of an alternative solution. Integrative thinking affords us, in the words of the poet Wallace Stevens, "the choice not between, but of."[7]

There's no reason to think that integrative thinking can be brought to bear only on the problems of business. In chapter 4, I discuss how Martha Graham used integrative thinking to rescue the art of the dance from sterile classicism and bring it to the center of the twentieth century's artistic revolution. Integrative thinking has also produced innovations in politics and policy. After World War II, U.S. diplomat George F. Kennan used his opposable mind to find a solution to the seemingly impossible problem of the Soviet Union. Faced with the expansionist ambitions of

Joseph Stalin, the United States appeared to have to choose between all-out war—unthinkable in the nuclear age—and acquiescence to Soviet empire building. But Kennan rejected both unacceptable alternatives and instead devised the U.S. policy of containment. Resisting Stalin's expansionist tendencies with a mixture of culture, diplomacy, economic pressure, military deterrence, and proxy forces, the containment doctrine steered the United States and the West between the poles of war and surrender and contributed significantly to the Soviet Union's eventual collapse. With its rejection of static, binary end-states in favor of complex, dynamic systems, containment has all the hallmarks of a product of integrative thinking.

The examples of Graham and Kennan suggest that integrative thinking can point us toward solutions not yet imagined to such profound problems as terrorism, global warming, and gross economic inequality. This book isn't the place to tackle those problems. But in describing how some of the best minds in business used integrative thinking to find profitable and innovative resolutions to seemingly irresolvable conflicts, perhaps this book can suggest new ways to approach some of today's—and tomorrow's—most pressing dilemmas.

All the Comforts of Home

Integrative thinking is what enabled Isadore Sharp to found and build the largest and most successful chain of luxury hotels in the world, Four Seasons Hotels and Resorts Ltd., whose brand is synonymous in guests' minds with the ultimate in luxury service. Sharp's first lodging property, a smallish roadside motel outside the core of downtown Toronto, was anything but the model for a present-day Four Seasons. Neither was one of his next projects, a large convention hotel in the heart of downtown Toronto. The two properties represented the two dominant models prevailing at the time in the worldwide hotel business.

Sharp found himself increasingly frustrated by the business propositions underlying both prevailing models. He loved the intimacy and comfort of his small motel, but with only one hundred twenty-five rooms, it didn't generate enough revenue to cover the cost of the workout facilities, meeting rooms, restaurants, and other amenities that business travelers valued. By the same token, he loved that his big convention hotel could provide its guests with every amenity they could desire. But with sixteen hundred rooms, it couldn't offer the personal touches that made his motel such an agreeable place to stay.

The two types of lodging stood in fundamental and apparently irreconcilable conflict. Guests could choose the small motel's intimacy and comfort or the large hotel's location and range of amenities, but no hotel could offer the best of both worlds. So just about everyone in the lodging business chose one type or another and accepted the drawbacks that came with their choice. But not Issy Sharp. Rather than choose one model or the other, each with its attendant shortcomings, Sharp used his opposable mind to create a new model, a hotel with the intimacy of his original motor inn and the amenities of a large convention hotel.

Solving the Pricing Paradox at P&G

When Procter & Gamble CEO A. G. Lafley took the helm in June of 2000, the venerable consumer products maker was floundering. Its growth had slowed almost to a standstill, and two consecutive quarterly profit warnings had finished the tenure of his predecessor. Seven of its top ten brands were suffering market-share declines. The company was spending more and more on research and development but introducing fewer and fewer innovations. It had lost touch with the consumer.

Much of the well-meaning advice people both inside and outside P&G offered Lafley proceeded from the assumption that the company's costs were out of control. This school of thought saw store brands and other low-cost alternatives as P&G's primary competitive threat, and low prices as P&G's logical competitive response. Drastic cost cuts were necessary to make the low prices sustainable. Lafley didn't necessarily disagree.

An opposing school of thought, meanwhile, held that P&G had stopped innovating. The only route to success, to this way of thinking, was to use innovation to differentiate P&G from its cut-price competitors, charge premium prices, and restore profitability. Lafley saw the sense of that argument as well. His easiest course would have been to tell employees, retailers, and consumers that P&G had opted for one alternative or the other: low costs and aggressively low pricing or intensive innovation investment, sharp brand differentiation, and premium pricing.

Like Lee-Chin, Lafley chose neither—and both. He concluded that P&G needed to pare costs and become more price-competitive. But he also concluded that P&G needed to emphasize the innovation that would make the company's brands clearly superior to the competition's. Over the next several years, Lafley eliminated layers of management, cut the size of functional units at the corporate level, outsourced where outsiders were more cost-effective, promoted inspiring young managers, stressed the importance of capability-building, and instilled through the organization a relentless focus on generating cash and cutting costs. At the same time, he tirelessly communicated his passion for delighting customers and delivering superior value to them. For the first time in P&G's history, design became a point of emphasis, and Lafley pioneered a new approach to innovation that strengthened the company's brands, enabling P&G to charge more for products than it had ever charged before. Before long, P&G was selling soaps, detergents, and toiletries at prices attractive in relation to those of store brands and discount offerings. At the same time, the company was introducing premium products like Olay Regenerist skin cream, which cost an unheard-of $25 for a three-ounce bottle.

What kind of mind could weave together a unified strategy from two such different lines of thought? An innocuous-sounding comment from Lafley furnishes an important clue. "I'm not an either-or kind of guy," he told me once. The results of thinking in terms of "and" rather than "or" have been breathtaking. Lafley has led P&G to consistently strong organic revenue growth, double-digit profit growth, and a doubling of the company's stock price within four years. In doing so, Lafley has established himself as one of the finest CEOs of his era.[8]

The Software Synthesis

In 1995, when Red Hat Inc. was posting sales of a mere $14 million, it didn't look like a company destined to grow into the world's dominant provider of Linux software, with annual revenue of $400 million, making cofounder Bob Young a billionaire in the process. In those days, the choices available to software entrepreneurs like Young seemed limited to two dominant business models. Companies such as Microsoft and Oracle typified the classic proprietary software model. They invested heavily in re-search and development, guarded their intellectual property jeal-ously, and charged high prices. They enjoyed wide profit margins because their customers, lacking access to the source code neces-sary to change or upgrade the software, were essentially locked into purchasing regular upgrades.

The alternative model was the so-called free software model— a misnomer, in that the software was cheap but not free. Suppliers of free software sold shrink-wrapped CD-ROMs that included both software and source code. Prices were modest—$15 for a copy of Slackware in the early days of Linux, versus $200 for Mi-crosoft Windows—but suppliers made money each time a new version was released. Volume was high, profit margins were thin, and revenue was uncertain, in part because the proliferation of small, idiosyncratic players scared away corporate customers who were looking for standardization and predictability.

Young deemed both models unsatisfactory. He found the high-margin, proprietary model distasteful because he was ideologically committed to the open software movement and its flagship, Linux. Linux and open software were predicated on the source code being freely available to all, giving Linux customers a degree of control over their software that the existing proprietary operating system suppliers were not willing to offer. But the orthodox free-software model placed unacceptable constraints on Red Hat's growth, mar-ket penetration, and profitability. If Red Hat simply followed the es-tablished model, it would be just one of many sellers of Linux-based operating systems and far from the biggest of a diverse lot. It would be locked into competing against a wide variety of developers, all of them producing a commodity product in a fringe market.

Faced with two existing options, neither of them terribly appealing, Young incorporated aspects of each: as a loyal soldier in the open-source movement, he decided that Red Hat's software would continue to be free. But like the proprietary software giants, Red Hat would profit by establishing an ongoing service relationship with its customers. Young reengineered Red Hat's software to make it available as a free download over the Internet. That one move, which sowed panic among his colleagues when he proposed it, vaulted it ahead of all its Linux rivals and established it as the only Linux provider of sufficient scale to gain the trust of big corporations. That corporate support established Red Hat's dominance and assured its financial strength.[9]

Doing or Thinking?

In this book, I analyze the process of integrative thinking, break it down into its constituent elements, and discuss the capacities and skills that people must develop to practice integrative thinking and exploit the full potential of the opposable mind. But before embarking on that exploration, it might be helpful to offer a working definition of integrative thinking:

> *The ability to face constructively the tension of opposing ideas and, instead of choosing one at the expense of the other, generate a creative resolution of the tension in the form of a new idea that contains elements of the opposing ideas but is superior to each.*

This thinking discipline was the most common feature I found among the numerous leaders I interviewed. But apart from the skillful and advanced use of the opposable mind, this group was remarkably diverse: they were older and younger; more overtly cerebral and more plainspoken; more aggressive and more laid-back; more gregarious and more reserved.

With so many differences among them, it would be presumptuous, at the very least, for me to claim to have found the *one thing* that guarantees leadership success. I am certain that a variety of capabilities contribute to business success. Intelligence, drive, and good health all play a part. So does getting the right break at the right time. But if nothing else, integrative thinking improves the odds of success, without foreclosing other actions and disciplines that other business thinkers rely on to solve problems.

My emphasis on thinking is not necessarily widely shared by business theorists and practitioners. In recent years, the dominant question addressed for the would-be leader is "What should I do?" rather than "What should I think?" To this way of thinking, the dot-com bust was largely a failure of grandiose strategies, and the collapse of the dot-coms tilted the conversation away from thinking to doing. The bias toward action is easily discerned in the three of the most influential business leadership books of recent years: *Execution: The Discipline of Getting Things Done* by Honeywell CEO Larry Bossidy and consultant Ram Charan; *Good to Great: Why Some Companies Make the Leap . . . and Others Don't* by professor-turned-guru Jim Collins; and *Jack: Straight from the Gut* by Jack Welch, the former super-CEO of GE General Electric Company.[10]

In *Execution*, Bossidy and Charan argue that "Execution is *the* great unaddressed issue in the business world today" and speak dismissively of executives who prefer to think about strategy. Bossidy and Charan itemize and specify all the things that executives must do to meet their definition of execution. The list gets pretty long: "The heart of execution lies in the three core processes: the people process, the strategy process, and the operations process . . . These processes are where the things that matter about execution need to be decided." [11] The rest of the book is dedicated to detailing what executives should do to execute within the three core processes, illustrated with the stories of impeccable execution by notable CEOs such as Dick Brown of EDS and Henry Schacht of Lucent Technologies.

In *Good to Great*, Collins seeks to explain how companies can go from being merely good to sustainably great. While doing that, he introduces the now-popular idea of "Level 5 Leadership," which is the kind of leadership found at companies that sustain greatness. Level 5 leaders, Collins argues, show a combination of determination and self-effacement. They relentlessly give credit to those around them instead of taking it themselves. They get the right people in the organization, give them jobs suited to their capabilities, and set aggressive goals. The book provides an extensive recipe for what one must do to be a Level 5 leader.

Welch's book takes the reader on a journey through his career, with the primary focus on what he did to reach the top of GE and what he did once he got there.

All three books stress action over strategy and describe the mindset that produces effective action. For Bossidy and Charan, the leaders' minds must be focused on execution and following through, to the exclusion of almost everything else. Collins's ideal mindset combines fierce will with personal humility. The mindset that Welch advocates is consumed with aiming high and settling for nothing less than winning.

I would never dispute the importance of doing: thinking without doing is of little value or consequence. However, even on their own terms, it is difficult to come away from those three best sellers with a compelling and practical prescription for what the would-be leader ought to do.

Following the logic of Bossidy and Charan is a challenge. Despite scoffing at leaders who focus on strategy rather than execution, they end up conceding that strategy is integral to execution. Because they cannot maintain a meaningful distinction between strategy and execution, the thing they call "execution" quickly morphs into a laundry list of everything a leader must do: strategy plus operations plus people management. Their theory is also undermined by the fate of the executives they chose as exemplars of superior execution. Shortly after the publication of the book, Brown and Schacht both were fired for dreadful performance.

After *Execution*, Collins's advice is refreshingly restrained and straightforward. He explains what a Level 5 leader does, but he freely admits that he can't yet tell readers how to become Level 5 leaders themselves. "For your own development," he writes, "I would love to be able to give you a list of steps for becoming Level 5, but we have no solid research data that would support a credible list."[12]

Welch is particularly interesting. He was one of my integrative thinker interviewees, and I came away seeing him as an exemplary integrative thinker. But I wouldn't advise trying to figure out how he thinks from what he did. Early in his tenure as GE's CEO, Welch insisted that each of GE's businesses be number one or number two in market share in its industry. He eventually noticed that his business unit leaders gamed the system he created by defining their markets in such a way that they were guaranteed the number one or two spot. Later in his career, he insisted that his businesses define their market share to be lower than 10 percent. He figured that business leaders would be quicker to spot market opportunities if they envisioned their market as much larger than their share of it. In this respect, Welch is an exemplary integrative thinker, secure enough to encounter changing circumstances without an inflexible ideology, and adaptable enough to change his approach when presented with new data. But emulating what Jack Welch *did* would invite confusion and incoherence, since Welch pursued diametrically opposed courses at different points in his career.

I don't wish to denigrate any of the books I've mentioned. They were best sellers for a reason: businesspeople want to know what makes a great leader because they themselves would like to be better leaders. Each book offers a particular perspective, and each perspective is valuable. But to approach every business problem with the question, "What should I do?" is to foreclose options before they can even be explored.

Bossidy and Charan demonstrate that a bias toward doing doesn't necessarily promote precise thinking. It can also promote a definition of execution that is too broad to be useful, crowding the entire spectrum of business activities under a single umbrella term. Collins demonstrates that even if you are pretty certain what Level 5 leaders do, there is no resultant prescription for what you should do to become a Level 5 leader. Finally, Welch demonstrates that a focus on leadership actions is limited because actions appropriate in one context can be completely inappropriate in another.

Instead of attempting to learn from observing the actions of leaders, I prefer to swim upstream to the antecedent of doing: thinking. My critical question is not what various leaders did, but how their cognitive processes produced their actions. Dick Brown's and

Henry Schacht's actions might have looked meritorious to Bossidy because something about them suggested good execution (however that may be defined). But their thinking produced actions that were a bad fit within their particular business context, leading to the failures that cost them their jobs.

Meet the Cast

Deciphering how exemplary managerial leaders *think* is the burden of this book. To do so, I picked leaders with unquestioned records of success. I strove to include a wide variety of leaders from a broad range of contexts. I included business rock stars such as Jack Welch, A. G. Lafley, Bob Young, and Meg Whitman of eBay, as well as less celebrated but equally successful CEOs, including Isadore Sharp, Chuck Knight of Emerson Electric, John Bachmann of Edward Jones, and Tim Brown of IDEO. I included a quintet of CEOs from fantastically successful Indian multinationals—Nandan Nilekani of Infosys Technologies, K. V. Kamath of ICICI Bank, Ramalinga Raju of Satyam Computer Services, and F. C. Kohli and S. Ramadorai of Tata Consultancy Services—and CEOs of globally consequential nonprofit organizations, including Victoria Hale of the Institute for OneWorld Health and Piers Handling of the Toronto International Film Festival. Also on my list are artists such as designer Bruce Mau and filmmaker Atom Egoyan. Finally, I included academics such as Nobel Laureate Michael Spence and the twentieth century's greatest business guru, Peter Drucker. These business academics have shifted the paradigms in their disciplines as profoundly as the CEOs on my list changed paradigms in their industries.

My approach was to explore in detail the thinking behind the decisions that each leader found particularly difficult to make. It is in those critical incidents, I believe, that thinking patterns are most clearly revealed. My exploration turned out to be a challenging process, for them as well as for me. One person I interviewed told me that my questions made his head hurt! I came to understand that many of those I interviewed thought about their choices in implicit or tacit ways. For many, their interviews with me marked the first time anyone had probed them on the thinking behind their most critically important decisions. Even though they were brilliant thinkers, they were not always reflective or articulate about their thought processes.

I interviewed most of them a single time, typically before a large audience. Almost all allowed their interviews to be videotaped. With two subjects, I performed much more detailed explorations, taping them for approximately eight hours. I did so to see if the shape of their thinking changed substantially with prolonged probing. It did not—I simply took away a deeper understanding of their thought patterns.

The interviews were exciting for me, but unsettling. I knew that my subjects came from widely differing backgrounds and reached success by a variety of routes. I didn't know when I started out if I would discern common patterns in their thinking. But the more interviews I conducted, the more strongly I came to feel that my interviewees' mental processors were equipped with a common operating system. They each used their operating system in their own unique context to produce their own unique outcome, but the thinking process seemed to come from a common program. The pattern of reasoning, or perhaps better, the cognitive discipline, that I discovered is what I came to call integrative thinking. It has a series of identifiable steps. It has a consistent purpose. It can be understood clearly and put into practice.

It is important to note at this point that not all successful business leaders are adept at integrative thinking. It was a common theme, not a universal one. Some of my sample group thought in ways that were distinct from the common pattern. And I freely admit that I couldn't figure out how certain leaders thought or how their thinking pattern contributed to success. From this I conclude that integrative thinking is not a necessary condition for success. Success can derive from other approaches. Within those limitations, however, the integrative thinking approach was the most common theme connecting the leaders I interviewed.

Cultivating the Opposable Mind

An important question remains: is the capacity for integrative thinking a gift reserved for a small minority or can it be consciously and intentionally developed? The Fitzgerald quote that opens this chapter suggests that integrative thinking is a naturally occurring capability limited to those born with "a first-rate intelligence." By contrast, Chamberlin, with his explicitly developmental perspective, implies that integrative thinking is a skill and discipline that even those of us who aren't geniuses can develop. In Chamberlin's view, the opposable mind is there waiting to be used—and with use, it develops its capacity for creating solutions that would otherwise not be evident:

The use of the method leads to certain peculiar habits of mind which deserve passing notice, since as a factor of education its disciplinary

value is one of importance. When faithfully pursued for a period of years,
it develops a habit of thought analogous to the method itself, which
may be designated a habit of parallel or complex thought. Instead of a
simple succession of thoughts in linear order, the procedure is complex,
and the mind appears to become possessed of the power of simultane-
ous vision from different standpoints. Phenomena appear to become
capable of being viewed analytically and synthetically at once.[13]

Is integrative thinking unteachable, or is it merely untaught? Is it
a function of pure intelligence, as Fitzgerald would have it, or of
dedication and practice, as Chamberlin suggests?

My own classroom experience suggests—but does not prove—
that people can be taught to use their opposable minds, and they
grow more skilled and confident with practice. But it is already
clear that integrative thinking is *untaught*. The world has not organized itself to produce integrative thinkers as it does brain sur-
geons or computer engineers. Integrative thinking is largely a tacit
skill in the heads of people who have cultivated, knowingly or
otherwise, their opposable minds. Many of those people don't appear to know how they are thinking or that it is different from the
common run of thought. They just do it. But an outsider can observe, describe, and analyze their thinking processes. And from this
conscious, systematic study, a method of teaching that process is
starting to emerge.

In the next chapter, I begin the exploration of integrative thinking by breaking that thinking process into its four constituent parts:
salience, causality, architecture, and resolution (chapter 2). Then I
show how integrative thinkers' capacity for distinguishing models
from reality is critical to driving through the constituent parts to a
creative resolution (chapter 3). Following that, I identify how the

twin forces of simplification and specialization discourage integrative thinking and describe how those forces can be countered (chapter 4). Then I introduce a framework for building integrative thinking capacity (chapter 5). Finally, I describe how to build capacity in each of the three components of the framework—stance (chapter 6), tools (chapter 7), and experiences (chapter 8)—including how each can be and is being taught.

CHAPTER 2

No Stomach for Second-Best

How Integrative Thinkers
Move Beyond Trade-offs

We weren't going to win if it was an "or." Everybody can do
"or." That's the way the world works. You trade things off but
you're not going to be the best in your industry. You are not
going to win if you are in a trade-off game.[1]

—A. G. Lafley, Chairman and CEO, Procter & Gamble

HOW DO INTEGRATIVE thinkers actually think? How do they consider the options before them in a way that leads forward to new possibilities and not merely back to the same inadequate alternatives? To answer those questions, let's look first at the cognitive steps we take in making a decision. We're rarely conscious of them as we work our way through them, but we engage in them whenever we make a decision, whether or not we employ integrative thinking. Which is to say that it's not the steps that set integrative thinkers apart; it's how they take them. But we need to understand the steps before we can see what integrative thinkers do differently.

The Process of Thinking and Deciding

Imagine you're planning your next summer holiday. After much thought and discussion with your spouse, you've whittled a nearly infinite number of choices down to three serious alternatives: touring Tuscany by bicycle, exploring the ancient Buddhist temples of Cambodia, or whale watching in Hawaii. As you and your spouse try to choose among three alternatives that seem equally compelling, you ask each other a series of questions:

- How much will each trip cost?

- What kinds of accommodations are available?

- What sorts of tours are offered? Can we find knowledge-able guides?

- Which destination is the most exotic and likely to offer the most unusual experiences?

- Will we learn something new on the trip?

- How safe is each alternative likely to be?

- How much time will we spend in transit, compared to the time we'll spend at our destination?

All those questions touch on the features that you and your spouse consider relevant and important, or *salient*, to your decision.

Other features will have no relevance or importance to you—or you won't recognize their relevance—and thus won't be salient in your decision-making process. For example, when you planned your trip, perhaps you didn't take into consideration the kinds of people you were likely to meet. You didn't intentionally leave that consideration out of your set of salient items. It just wasn't on your mental desktop when you were making your holiday plans—something you may regret when you find yourself sharing a tour bus with a party of hard-drinking hardware salespeople and their chatty spouses. Salience is individual and idiosyncratic; what I see as salient might be completely different from what you see as salient. And both of us have blind spots that make it likely, though not certain, that something important will be left off our list of salient concerns. "I wish I'd thought of that sooner" is just another way of saying, "I wish that had been salient to me when I was making up my mind."

Having selected our salient features, however imperfectly, we next consider how they relate to one another: The word we give to the pattern formed by the relationships is *causality*. Will a long trip cost more than a short one (i.e., is there a causal relationship between the length of a trip and its cost)? Is a potential destination less safe because it's more exotic? Will my traveling companions enhance my experience or make me regret signing up for the tour? In essence, we build a little map in our heads as to how the salient features influence one another—that is, their causal relationship to each other. A causal map lays out the array of causal relationships at work in a given situation.

With the causal map of salient features in our mind, we turn to the *architecture* of the decision. In simple decisions, the architecture is minimal because the decision is binary: "Shall I go to the newly released blockbuster movie tonight, or stay in and watch television?" Our vacation decision, on the other hand, has multiple moving parts: travel, lodging, and activities, just for starters. We might say to ourselves: "I am going to think first about what tours are available at each destination before I worry about hotels and flight schedules and fares." Alternatively, we might think: "I am going to figure out the cost and logistics of getting there before I even think about what I can do when I get there." Either sequence is reasonable. You might also break up the job, looking at flight schedules and lodging options while your spouse searches the tours available at each destination.

There are various paths a decision might take; none is necessarily right or wrong. But you'll probably resist trying to keep the whole vacation problem in mind as you and your spouse work out its constituent parts. Keeping the whole in mind makes your head hurt. So instead you'll keep each component of your decision in its own separate compartment. That eases the mental burden, but it might also mean that you lose half a day of sightseeing because you opt for the earliest, cheapest flight home. A later and only slightly more expensive flight would allow you a few more hours to tour a vineyard, visit another temple, or check out the whaling museum, but because you're focused on only one part of the problem—the price—you overlook the effect your choice has on the overall experience.

Finally you choose: you come to a *resolution* as to whether you'll roll through Tuscany, trek through Cambodia, or ply the waters off Hawaii. Or maybe none of your three options was satisfactory—the flight schedules were inconvenient, the lodging was substandard, the tours were all booked—and you begin the decision-making process again from the beginning. The diagram in figure 2-1 represents that thinking process graphically. Note that it allows for discarding your set of alternatives and starting over, which is why the dotted arrows in the diagram head back down the cascade.

Whatever we decide, we'll arrive at our choice by considering a set of features we deem *salient*; creating a mental model of the *causal relationships* among those features; arranging those causal relationships into an *architecture* intended to produce a specific outcome; thereby reaching a *resolution* of the problem at hand. With different salience, causality, and architecture, we would almost certainly arrive at a different outcome.

Now that we've broken the decision-making process into four steps, let's revisit the question with which we began this chapter: How do integrative thinkers actually think? To answer that question, let's observe an integrative thinker as he works his way toward a business decision.

FIGURE 2-1

The process of thinking and deciding

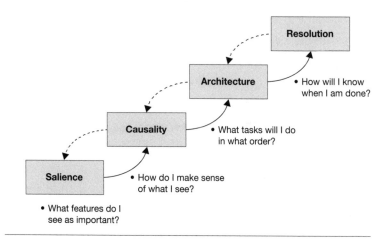

Isadore Sharp: Creating the Four Seasons Difference

Meet Isadore Sharp, one of four children of Polish parents who immigrated to Toronto before his birth in 1931.[2] His father, a plasterer by trade, became a contractor. Issy, as he is known to his friends, was a star athlete in high school, where he was known as "Razzle-Dazzle Issy," and helped his father on jobs as a teenager.

After college, he worked at his father's construction company. While he was building a motel for a client, he formed the ambition of building and running a motel of his own. Six years later, after endless rejections by lenders and developers, Sharp finally secured funding for his project from friends and family. The Four Seasons Motor Hotel opened in 1961 with 125 rooms in a rather seedy area outside the core of downtown Toronto. A standard room cost about $12 a night.[3]

When Sharp began his undertaking, would-be hoteliers had two choices. They could build a small motel with fewer than two hundred rooms and offer guests modest amenities—often not much more than a television set in the room, an ice machine down the hall, and a bar and restaurant in the lobby. The capital requirements of such an establishment were modest and per-room operating costs were low. The Four Seasons Motor Hotel followed that model. With its warm, intimate atmosphere, friendly service, and welcoming restaurant and bar, it became a favorite watering hole for local businesspeople.

The alternative to the small, few-frills motels was the large downtown hotel catering to business travelers. Such hotels usually had at least seven hundred fifty guest rooms and extensive amenities, including conference facilities, multiple restaurants, and banquet rooms. (More recently, such hotels have added fitness centers, business centers, and teleconferencing facilities.) Sharp's fourth hotel, a sixteen hundred-room downtown convention hotel with extensive amenities, including a huge shopping arcade, met that description. Like Sharp's first motel, it was profitable and popular.

Each type of hotel had its advantages, as well as distinct drawbacks. For all its comfort and intimacy, the small motel simply wasn't an option for the business traveler who needed a well-appointed meeting room or state-of-the-art communications facilities. Large hotels produced a big enough pool of revenues to fund the amenities the market demanded, but they tended to be cold and impersonal places; it was easy for guests to feel anonymous and fungible.

After opening that fourth hotel in 1972, Four Seasons Sheraton, Sharp mulled his next move. He loved his cozy little Four Seasons Motor Hotel but realized it couldn't generate the revenue to maintain the amenities expected by his target market, well-heeled business travelers. He and his guests loved the amenities the Four Seasons Sheraton's cash flow afforded, but its sheer scale ensured that guests would never feel truly at home there.

Rather than choose one of the existing dominant models and accept the downside it entailed, Sharp used his opposable mind to hold the two models in his head, roll them around, and design a creative resolution of the tension between them. He sought, he told me, "to combine the best of the small hotel with the best of the large hotel." He envisioned a medium-sized hotel—big enough to bring an extensive array of amenities within range but smaller than the standard large hotel to maintain the sense of intimacy and personalized service.

He even had a prototype. His third hotel, London's Inn on the Park (now the Four Seasons) had been built under tough London space constraints. With 220 rooms and suites, it was smaller than a typical luxury hotel and gave Sharp a glimpse of the intimacy, luxury, and comfort possible on an in-between scale.

But the scale that made the Inn on the Park so attractive to Sharp and his guests also presented a seemingly insurmountable economic obstacle. The Inn would earn only anemic profits if it charged the same per room as competitors did, because it had to spread the cost of amenities over fewer rooms than other high-end hotels. But Sharp refused to be bound by the traditional economics of the hotel business. He reasoned that if the Four Seasons offered distinctly better service than its competitors, it could charge a substantial price premium, boosting revenue per room to the point where the hotel could afford top-of-the-line amenities. Before he could ask guests to pay a super-premium room rate, though, Sharp understood that Four Seasons Hotels would have to offer them an entirely different kind of service in return.

Salience at Four Seasons

What did an entirely different kind of service look and feel like? Answering that question meant thinking differently than the average hotelier. And thinking differently started with going beyond conventional notions of what was salient. Like other hoteliers, Sharp considered factors such as location, staffing levels, room size, and furnishings. But Sharp didn't stop there. He asked what his guests, mostly traveling business executives, were looking for when they booked a hotel room. His rivals recognized that businesspeople wanted to be treated well and catered to. Sharp's view of salience was more nuanced and humane. He understood that the vast majority of his guests traveled much more frequently than they ever would have wanted and that the experience they longed for most was to feel as if they were at home or at their office. They didn't want grand and formal. In Sharp's words:

> *We studied, surveyed, and listened to our customers. Most were business executives, often pressured by time and the need to be productive. Luxury, then, was seen chiefly as architecture and décor. We decided to redefine luxury as service—a support system to fill in for the one left at home and the office.*

Seeking to replicate that at-home feeling, Four Seasons was the first to offer shampoo in the shower, twenty-four-hour room service, bathrobes, makeup mirrors, hair dryers, overnight shoe shines, dry cleaning, and pressing. To make his guests feel more like they were in their own offices, Four Seasons was the first to install a two-line phone in every guest room, as well as a big, well-lighted desk. Four Seasons was also the first to provide twenty-four-hour secretarial services. In due course, rivals copied all of these initiatives, but not before Four Seasons established a reputation for providing service that its competitors couldn't match because it was literally unimaginable to them.

Also salient to Sharp was the structure of the hotel market in each new Four Seasons location. The traditional approach in the industry was to set a relatively fixed standard of physical and service quality across the entire chain. That simplified operations and made it easier to maintain a distinct brand identity.

Sharp, though, rejected the one-size-fits-all approach. Toronto was different from Chicago, which was different from New York, which was different from Paris. To be the number-one hotel in town, each city's Four Seasons would have to reflect what Sharp calls the local "color and culture." Its standard of quality would depend on the local context, even if matching the standard to the city created a much more complicated managerial challenge.

The results were worth the extra managerial effort. By taking the local market's structure and standards into account, Four Seasons is less likely than its rivals to overshoot or undershoot the local market in price and quality. The Four Seasons George V Hotel in Paris earns Zagat's rating as the best hotel in the world precisely because Sharp and his senior managerial team designed the hotel to embody Parisian standards of luxury, rather than some internal standard that doesn't recognize local differences.

Sharp, unlike his rivals, also recognized the salience of the hotel's ownership structure. To his rivals, operating and owning a hotel went hand in hand. But Sharp had learned from experience that ownership entailed as many drawbacks as benefits. Ownership tied up capital and exposed the hotelier to fluctuating local real estate values. It diverted valuable senior management time. Four Seasons shed those burdens by becoming the first big hotel company to manage, rather than own, the hotel facilities that bore its name. Investment groups would come to own all of Four Seasons' hotels, which Four Seasons manages under long-term contracts. As with the in-room amenities Four Seasons introduced, some competitors in due course copied Sharp, splitting their hotel management from hotel ownership. But Sharp got there first, because he saw salient features that his industry rivals overlooked.

Causality at Four Seasons

To carve out a distinctive identity for Four Seasons hotels, Sharp had to do more than take an expansive view of what was salient.

He also had to perceive causal relationships among points of salience that other hoteliers had overlooked.

Certain causal relationships are obvious to anyone in the hotel business. There's a clear relationship between room utilization and profitability, and between room revenue and food and beverage revenue. But Sharp saw other, more subtle causal relationships that escaped the notice of rival hoteliers.

Sharp saw a more complex relationship between hotel size and amenity level. The traditional belief, based on industry standard room rates and occupancy levels, was that a full-service business traveler hotel needed at least seven hundred fifty rooms to generate the revenue to pay for the amenities business travelers demanded. Sharp saw the causal relationship between scale and profitability a little differently. He understood that if he could give guests a good reason to pay significantly more per room per night, he could offer amenities at least as attractive as those of his rivals.

What would constitute a good enough reason to pay a lofty premium? Service that was different from other hotels not just in degree, but in kind. And how could Sharp attain that level of service? By seeing the causal link between the way a hotel treated its employees and the way employees treated their guests, and making that link the cornerstone of the Four Seasons brand.

Traditionally, managers in the hotel industry view employees as disposable. Turnover is very high, and employee payroll, the biggest variable cost by far, is the first thing cut during economic downturns. Most hotel workers come to see themselves as management sees them: as short-term, interchangeable parts whose employment could end tomorrow.

Although there's little loyalty or sense of shared purpose on either side of the equation, most employees do what's asked of them.

Their job security, such as it is, depends on adhering to certain rules and standards. Hence the causal relationship as understood by both management and employees is that good service is a matter of meeting fixed, context-independent standards—which just might explain the mechanical quality of the courtesy extended by many hotel employees. What's more, good service isn't an end in itself but a means to continued employment.

Sharp had a different idea of how to motivate and discipline employees. He saw a direct causal relationship between employees who felt well-treated by their employer and guests who felt well-treated by hotel employees. "Employees believed only what they saw," he told me. "If we were seen showing greater concern for profit, prestige, quotas, rather than for customers and employees, there'd be no belief in our values, no whole-hearted commitment."

Four Seasons set out to treat its employees far differently than the rest of the industry. To make them feel as permanent a part of Four Seasons as economically possible, Four Seasons went further than any other chain to retain employees during downturns. It offered more employee training than any other chain. It sought to fill managerial jobs from within rather than by hiring from outside. According to Sharp, Four Seasons sought to be different "by hiring more for attitude than experience, by establishing career paths and promotion from within, by paying as much attention to employee complaints as guest complaints, by upgrading employee facilities whenever we upgraded a hotel, by disallowing class distinctions in cafeterias and parking lots, by pushing responsibility down and encouraging self-discipline, by setting performance high and holding people accountable, and most of all, adhering to our credo, generating trust."

Sharp's management has generated enough trust to establish Four Seasons as the employer of choice in the hotel industry. When the Four Seasons in New York City opened in 1994, more than thirty thousand people applied for four hundred jobs.[4] As of this writing, the company has appeared on *Fortune* magazine's list of the "Top 100 Companies to Work For" every year since the ranking first appeared in 1998.[5]

Architecture at Four Seasons

In designing his decision on Four Seasons' competitive strategy, Sharp did not proceed sequentially or dole out separate pieces of the strategy-making to various functional areas. Instead of first deciding how big a hotel would be, then establishing service standards, and then setting human resources policy, he kept the chain of considerations firmly, clearly, and centrally in mind while working on individual links in the chain.

One organizing principle, or "credo" as Sharp calls it, runs through the entire Four Seasons organization. Everyone at the Four Seasons is guided by "the Golden Rule: to deal with others—partners, customers, coworkers, everyone—as we would want them to deal with us." This of course is not a novel concept—it's taught by countless parents to countless children around the world (with, of course, variable effect). The novelty was Sharp's decision to make it the bedrock management principle of a high-end hotel chain.

More than a management principle, however, the Golden Rule bound together all the parts of the strategy decisions at Four Seasons. Four Seasons senior management, beginning with the courtly, impeccably groomed Sharp, was going to treat its employees the way the managers themselves would want to be treated. And employees would respond by treating guests in the same spirit. Every phase of hotel operations would cohere around a strategy based on extraordinary service.

Plenty of companies pay lip service to the notion that people are their most important resource, but Sharp left no doubt that he meant it. "What was new was that we enforced it," he told me. "Senior managers who couldn't or wouldn't walk the talk were all whittled out within a few years. It was a painful process and personally distressing—perhaps the hardest thing I ever did. But the fastest way for management to destroy its credibility is to say employees come first and then to be seen putting them last. Better not to profess any values than not to live up to them."

To ensure that his entire operation remained focused on extraordinary guest service, Sharp issued one last, crucial decree: Four Seasons would have no customer service department. Instead of making customer service the responsibility of a discrete department, everyone at the Four Seasons was not just a member of the customer service department, but in charge of it.

Resolution at Four Seasons

Sharp arrived at a resolution that went above and beyond the two dominant models that had guided the decisions of other hoteliers, while incorporating significant elements of both. Sharp's resolution produced a system of reinforcing activities, each of which fits with and strengthens the whole, to outperform the dominant models in the industry (see figure 2-2).[6]

FIGURE 2-2

Four Seasons activity system

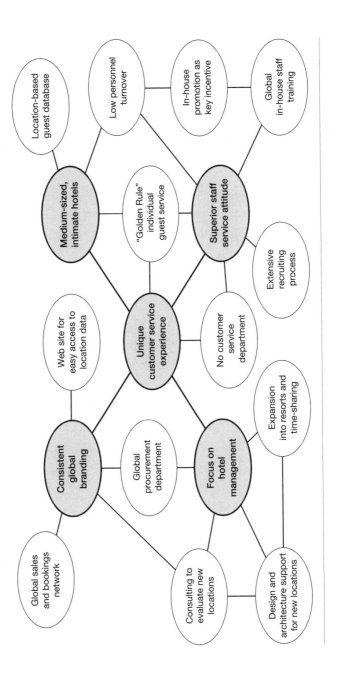

Sharp set out to create "a reputation for service so clear in people's mind that Four Seasons' name will become an asset of far greater value than bricks and mortar," and the results speak for themselves. With seventy-three hotels in thirty-one countries at last count, and with twenty-five properties under development, Four Seasons is considerably larger than the next biggest luxury player—Ritz-Carlton, with fifty-nine hotels. *Condé Nast Traveler* ranks eighteen Four Seasons hotels in its global Top 100 list, more than three times the next most cited chain. J. D. Power and Associates ranks Four Seasons first in luxury hotels. Zagat ranks the Four Seasons as the top U.S. hotel chain. Cities and countries send delegations to Sharp to plead with him to open a hotel in their locale, because a Four Seasons signifies that a city has become a global destination.

Sharp did nothing less than fashion a new way to succeed in the luxury lodging business. He would say he applied his experience and practical knowledge to the problem. But with all due respect to Sharp's long years in the business, plenty of people in the hotel industry have experience and know-how. Only Sharp came up with the Four Seasons business model. I would argue that the key difference between Sharp and other shrewd veterans of the lodging business was Sharp's willingness to consider a broader set of salient features, delve into more complicated causal relationships, and view the decision he was facing holistically. Those three features of his thinking pattern enabled him to find a way around the unpleasant trade-offs he faced.

Throughout Sharp's decision process, it's possible to discern clear differences between the mental mechanisms of integrative thinkers and those of conventional thinkers, and I go into those differences next. For the purpose of discussion, I posit a stark dichotomy between an integrative and conventional thinker, although it's more accurate to think of a spectrum that ranges from unadulterated integrative thinking to not-at-all integrative thinking. There's no intent in this discussion to disparage conventional thinkers, but rather to highlight the differences between them and integrative thinkers.

Embracing the Mess

The first difference between integrative thinkers and conventional thinkers is that integrative thinkers take a broader view of what is salient. Instrumental to Sharp's winning resolution was his choice to attend not just to the stated demands of his guests but also to their unstated but deeply held wish to be either at home or at their office. Because that wish was in his field of vision, he was able to take into consideration things his competitors couldn't—because they didn't know those things existed. When other luxury hotels put shampoo in their showers, it wasn't because they understood guests at a deeper level; it was because Four Seasons had done it and it seemed to work.

More salient features make for a messier problem. But integrative thinkers don't mind the mess. In fact, they welcome it, because the mess assures them that they haven't edited out features necessary to the contemplation of the problem as a whole. They welcome complexity because they know the best answers arise from complexity. And they feel confident that they will not get lost along the way but emerge on the other side of the problem with a clear resolution.

Second, integrative thinkers don't flinch from considering multidirectional and nonlinear causal relationships. Simple, unidirectional relationships are easier to hold in the mind, but they don't generate more satisfactory resolutions. So rather than simply think, "that competitor's price cutting is hurting our bottom line," the integrative thinker would conclude, "our product introduction really upset our competitors. Now they're cutting prices in response, and our profitability is suffering." In Sharp's case, he saw a more complicated relationship between hotel size and profitability than did the rest of the industry. Most people in the industry accepted that a minimum number of rooms was necessary to cover the cost of amenities and still provide an acceptable profit. Above that minimum, profit increased in a straight line with number of rooms. Sharp saw a more complex and nuanced relationship. He perceived an inverse relation between the number of rooms and his guests' feeling of comfort and intimacy—there were, in other words, both costs and benefits to increasing the number of rooms. His competitors saw only the benefits.

Sharp also saw a complex causal relationship between guest service quality and the way employees felt about their employer. Conventional thinkers in the hotel business believed that service quality depended on tight regulation of employee-guest interactions. Sharp saw a much different, nonlinear causal relationship. Employees who felt they belonged to a Four Seasons family that treated them according to the Golden Rule would be inspired to provide service well beyond the merely adequate. Employees who felt disposable wouldn't—couldn't—do more than what the service handbook required.

The third difference between integrative and conventional thinkers is in the architecture of their decisions. Integrative thinkers don't break a problem into independent pieces and work on each piece separately. They keep the entire problem firmly in mind while working on its individual parts. Integrative thinkers want to avoid the trap of designing a product before considering the costs of manufacturing it. So they would consider manufacturability as they design their product. Sharp used the Golden Rule as his central organizing principle. It touched every aspect of the strategy and illustrates his ability and insistence on keeping the whole in mind while working on the individual parts. In fact, Sharp describes the decision to make the Golden Rule the basis of all hotel operations as the choice that "bound together and made possible the other major choices."

As they do with salience and causality, integrative thinkers allow complexity to compound as they design their decisions. The complexity presents a cognitive challenge that integrative thinkers welcome, because they know that complexity brings along in its train an opportunity for a breakthrough resolution.

Fourth and finally, the integrative thinker will always search for creative resolution of tensions, rather than accept unpleasant trade-offs. The behaviors associated with such a search—delays, sending teams back to examine things more deeply, generating new options at the eleventh hour—can appear irresolute from the outside, but the results are choices that could only have been generated by an integrative thinker who won't settle for trade-offs and conventional options. Sharp longed to create a combination of "the best of a small motel and a large hotel." He didn't want to sacrifice one for the other and wasn't satisfied with either. The only way to accomplish his goal was to create a new-to-the-world model.

The distinctive features of integrative thinking are illustrated in figure 2-3.

FIGURE 2-3

The practices of integrative thinkers

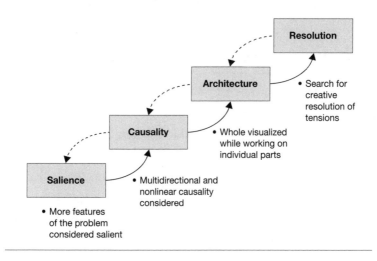

Conventional Thinking, or the
Art of Settling for Second-Best

The thinking that produces the vast majority of managerial decisions follows a very different approach to each of the four steps. The conventional goal in salience is to build the simplest possible map of the decision by discarding as many features as possible—or not even considering them in the first place. Organizational structures and cultures typically encourage simplification by promoting specialization. Each functional specialty has its own narrow view of what is salient. Until recently, finance departments never viewed emotional considerations as salient, and in turn, departments concerned with organizational behavior rarely regarded numerical and quantitative questions as salient. The members of those departments are pressured to pare away their views of what's salient until it matches the department's doctrine. In essence, then, departmental specialization conditions people to pay attention to only a subset of the many things to which they might otherwise productively pay attention.

We often implicitly recognize after the fact that our determination of salience was problematic. When decisions we make go badly, we think to ourselves, "I should have thought about how the wording of the memo would have been interpreted by the employees in our European operation," or "I should have thought about the state's road-repair program before siting our new distribution center." That's an acknowledgement of an error in salience. It's not that we incorrectly judged the salience of a feature. We didn't judge it salient at all. That's no accident. The complex organization of which we're a part is structured in such a way that many features of our environment are outside the purview of our job or functional specialty. Those are usually the features we fail to see as salient.

Conventional thinkers also tend to take a narrow and simplistic view of causality. The simplest of all is a straight-line causal relationship between dependent and independent variables. It's no accident that linear regression is the business world's preferred tool for establishing the relationship between one variable and another. Other tools are available, of course, but most managers shun them because it's easier to think about simple, unidirectional causal relationships. How many times has a superior scolded you for making a problem more complicated than it needs to be? You protest that you're not trying to complicate anything; you just want the problem to be as complicated as it really is. Your boss tells you to stick to your job, which involves taking a causal relationship rich with potential complexity and flattening it into a linear relationship in which more of A produces more of B.

When decisions go bad, sometimes it is because we got the causal links between salient features wrong. We could have gotten the direction of the relationship right but the magnitude wrong: "I thought that our costs would decrease much faster as our scale grew than they actually did." Or we could have gotten the direction of the relationship wrong: "I thought that our capacity to serve clients would go up when we hired a new batch of consultants, but it actually went down because the experienced consultants had to spend a huge amount of their time training the new consultants and fixing their rookie mistakes."

With respect to architecture, the most common failing of conventional thinking is the tendency to lose sight of the whole decision. It may be easier to dole out pieces of a decision to various corporate functions, but that ensures that no one will take a holistic view of a particular problem. And in the absence of a holistic view, a mediocre result is the likely outcome. Imagine if Sharp had delegated to four different executive vice presidents the questions of marketing, customer service, hotel operations, and human resources. Would their individual answers, bolted together into an overall Four Seasons strategy, have looked anything like the resolution that Sharp crafted? Almost certainly not.

Finally, with respect to resolution, conventional decision makers tend to accept unpleasant trade-offs with relatively little complaint. What alternative is there? By the time a decision maker reaches the resolution stage, the potential for discovering interesting and novel ways around unpleasant trade-offs has been leached away. So instead of rebelling against the unpleasant trade-off, the conventional thinker shrugs and asks, "What else could have we done?" Much else, in fact, could have been done, if the decision has been approached from a completely different direction, one that embraced complexity, multidirectional causal relationships, and holistic, rather than segmented, thinking.

The World as It Is, or as It Might Be?

The differences between integrative and conventional thinking are summarized in figure 2-4.

FIGURE 2-4

Integrative versus conventional thinking

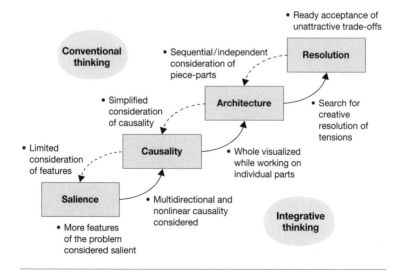

The two types of thinking are diametrically opposed, and so are the outcomes they generate. Integrative thinking produces possibilities, solutions, and new ideas. It creates a sense of limitless possibility. Conventional thinking hides potential solutions in places they can't be found and fosters the illusion that no creative solution is possible. With integrative thinking, aspirations rise over time. Conventional thinking is a self-reinforcing lesson that life is about accepting unattractive and unpleasant trade-offs. It erodes aspiration. Fundamentally, the conventional thinker prefers to accept the world as it is. The integrative thinker welcomes the challenge of shaping the world for the better.

CHAPTER 3

Reality, Resistance, and Resolution

How Integrative Thinkers
Keep Their Options Open

Reality is merely an illusion, albeit a very persistent one.

—Albert Einstein

IF INTEGRATIVE THINKING is such a good idea, why don't people use their opposable minds all the time? Craig Wynett, head of corporate new ventures at Procter & Gamble, answers with a great metaphor; he blames our "factory setting."[1] Like your car's ignition timing, your computer's screen brightness, or your washing machine's spin cycle, your mind emerges from the factory set for a specific mode and speed of operation. Few factory settings ever get adjusted, and many of us wouldn't know how to change them if we wanted to—hence all those VCRs forever flashing *12:00 a.m.* But as with your ignition timing, screen brightness, and spin cycle, your mind's setting can be adjusted, if you know how.

One factory preset of the human mind is a tendency to assume that our models of reality are identical to reality itself. That conflation shuts down the latent power of our opposable mind before it can be engaged. To understand how, let's look at how our minds process some of the data that swarms over and around us daily.

The World, Filtered

We swim in a veritable ocean of data every day. We don't drown in it because we are born with a capacity to shape it into something meaningful. But that meaning comes at the expense of a great deal of information. We filter out much of what comes flying at us and knock the rest into some kind of narrative order that seems to make sense. There's no guarantee that we won't filter out valuable data in our drive to compile a coherent narrative. As cognitive psychology professor Jordan Peterson puts it: "There's an infinite wealth of information in this room, yet when you come in and you process it, you only see those things that directly serve your purposes. The things you don't know, and the territories you don't know how to maneuver in, are everywhere."[2]

Close your eyes and picture the room you are in right now. You aren't seeing the room in its infinitely detailed reality. You are seeing a simplified model of the room that your mind has painted with a broad brush. Models are our customized understanding of reality.

We filter the data that besieges us in part to protect our brains. The thalamus is the part of the brain where incoming information is organized, and if it is disabled, "massive amounts of sensory information comes pouring through," says Peterson. "That's very,

very overwhelming, and that seems to be the reason, by the way, that people become schizophrenic. It's that too much of what's out there is pouring in, and their bodies cannot handle it, their exploratory systems burn out, and their conceptual systems start to fragment. Not a pretty thing."

Corporate *Rashomon*

Nor is it a pretty sight when we confuse our simplified models of reality with reality itself, in all its rich complexity. Here's an example of how our capacity for filtering information, meant to make sense of the world, can instead make for confusion and conflict.

Sally and Bill are two vice presidents of a real company, which we'll call VisionTech. Like the rest of us, Sally and Bill create narratives from the data that comes at them, and like the rest of us, they are prone to the mistaken belief that their narratives and reality are one and the same.[3]

Sally and Bill have just paid a visit to an important customer. During the visit, the customer said, *"I really like VisionTech. It has been an innovative leader in this business for a long time. But I'm coming under increasing cost pressure and have to make trade-offs."*

That's a verbatim statement, objective reality, tape-recorded and then transcribed by a third party who wasn't at the meeting. Our minds' factory settings come into play when we unconsciously extract from that reality the information that has salience to us and fit it into a coherent story. Sally zeroed in on the first and second sentences of the customer's statement (*"I really like VisionTech. It has been an innovative leader in this business for a long time"*) and all but forgot the rest (*"But I'm coming under increasing cost pressure and have to make trade-offs"*). Her memory was accurate, as far as it went. The words came out of the customer's mouth in the order she remembered. But because she didn't recognize the back half of the customer's statement as salient, it found no place in her mental model.

Reality and Sally's model of reality start to diverge when she tries to interpret the causal content embedded in the customer's statement. According to her interpretation, the customer is really telling her and Bill that he places a high value on VisionTech's leadership and innovation.

What has changed? "Liking" VisionTech has been replaced with "valuing" VisionTech's leadership and innovation. But "liking" and "valuing" mean different things. Customers may like lots of things, but they pay for—that is, they value—only a small subset of the things they like. By changing "like" to "value," Sally has added a causal relationship—this customer will pay us for the fruits of our leadership—that wasn't in the customer's original statement. Sally then fits this newly processed data, which she would call a fact, into the narrative she's made of her past experience. Her conclusion: *"Customers value VisionTech's leadership and innovation."* And that conclusion, in turn, points toward a general causal relationship: *"Customers will stick with us if we continue to innovate and lead."* Finally, Sally uses her model to plot a way forward for VisionTech, based on what she believes customers think: *"Innovation and leadership are the most critical avenues to pursue."*

Sally's resolution is based on a mental construction, not on objective reality. She has taken real data that she found salient and added layers and layers of causal interpretations to fashion a prescription for what VisionTech should and should not do to meet

ressure." Which in turn leads to the following conclu-
omers will migrate away from us because of our pricing." Just
d, Bill in due course comes to an ultimate resolution as
ction VisionTech must take, predicated on his interpre-
what customers think: "We've got to get our costs down so
n be price competitive."

Bill's thinking model contrasts with Sally's is illustrated in
-2.

divergent narratives that Sally and Bill have constructed
equally plausible. Both proceed from objective data. But
sulting resolutions are polar opposites. That's not unusual.
less data combined with the mind's natural drive to add mean-
roduce a profusion of clashing models.

URE 3-2

dels and resolutions: Sally versus Bill

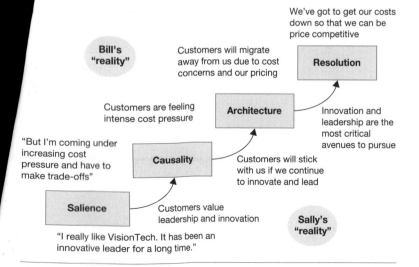

what she believes are the core co
(see figure 3-1).

Sally's model turns out the way
setting. But settings are nonstandar
same models from the same set of da
the same customer statement and can
different sense of its meaning. The pa
registered as salient was, *"But I'm comin*
sure and have to make trade-offs."

Starting from that slice of salient reality,
distinctly different direction. He infers that
to make a trade-off against VisionTech beca
From there, Bill constructs a generalization:

intense cost
sion: *"Cu*
as Sally di
to what a
tation of
that we c
How
figure
The
appea
the re
Limi
ing

FIG

M

FIGURE 3-1

Sally's thinking process

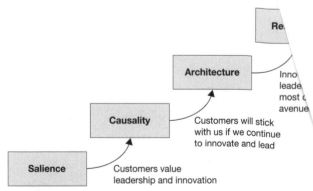

Re

Architecture

Inno
leade
most
avenue

Causality

Customers will stick
with us if we continue
to innovate and lead

Salience

Customers value
leadership and innovation

"I really like VisionTech. It has been an
innovative leader for a long time."

But Sally doesn't see her construction as a model of reality—she sees it as reality itself. As she told me at a debriefing after the meeting with the customer, her narrative is "the way it is in our industry." Bill, too, insisted to me that his view was "reality."

On their way back to VisionTech headquarters, Sally and Bill talk over their meeting with the customer. Bill says, "We risk losing our client base if we don't get our costs down."

Sally is flabbergasted. *"What client interview was Bill at?"* she wonders to herself. *"Or does he have an agenda that causes him to completely ignore the customers and push cost cutting, which is exactly the opposite of what they want?"* Aloud, she says, "But Bill, our clients are counting on us to show leadership in innovation."

Bill can't believe his ears. *"Was Sally at the same meeting I was?"* he thinks. *"Or does she have a hidden agenda that leads her to completely ignore the customers' wishes and push for innovation, whatever it costs? That is exactly the opposite of what they want!"*

When Opposites Collide

The communication breakdown between Sally and Bill is a consequence of their conflating their mental models with reality. Both exhibit a strong tendency to defend their own models of reality and disparage any model that clashes with it. "We think that what we see," says John Sterman, MIT's expert in systems thinking, "is what there really is."[4]

This tendency makes it difficult for us to know what to do with opposing and seemingly incommensurable models. Our first impulse is to determine which one represents reality and which one is unreal and wrong, and then we campaign against the idea we reject. But in rejecting one model as unreal, we miss out on all the value that can be realized by holding in mind two opposing models at the same time. We disengage the opposable mind before it can seek a creative resolution.

The integrative thinkers I interviewed have learned to change their factory settings and distinguish between reality and models that purport to reflect reality. Unlike the rest of us, they don't need to take sides. "It's not a choice of this model or that model," says Sterman. "They're all wrong. See what you can do to combine those multiple perspectives and enhance the quality of your mental model."

Let's now look at three extraordinary executives who each demonstrate the capacity to hold multiple perspectives in mind at the same time and still function. These leaders—A. G. Lafley, CEO of Procter & Gamble; Bob Young, cofounder and builder of Red Hat software; and Piers Handling, the visionary behind the global emergence of the Toronto International Film Festival—demonstrate the power that comes from distinguishing mental models from reality. Later in the book, I discuss how you can go about changing your factory setting to do the same.

How A. G. Lafley Reinvented Innovation at P&G

When A. G. Lafley took over as CEO of Procter & Gamble in 2000, the company had just warned Wall Street for the second time in two quarters that it would miss its profit targets. Growth was slowing, profits were sliding, and many of its biggest brands were losing market share. P&G's stock price had fallen nearly 50 percent in six months, and the business press was openly questioning whether P&G had lost its long-standing eminence in consumer goods marketing. The front-page headline for industry bible *Advertising Age* read: "Does P&G Still Matter?"[5]

By P&G's conservative standards, the fifty-three-year-old Lafley was young for the top job, although he was then a twenty-three-year veteran of the company—a "lifer"—with an impressive record of innovation. He had overseen the launch of liquid Tide, Tide with bleach, and compact Tide—all successful extensions of P&G's flagship brand. As head of P&G's Asia operation, he and his small team transformed SKII, a tiny skin care brand originally distributed only in Japan and Hong Kong, into a global prestige brand. In the process, sales grew by a factor of twenty. But because Lafley's predecessor had just earned the dubious distinction of being the first CEO in the company's one hundred seventy-year history to be fired, Lafley was thrust into the CEO post without the formal grooming that was customary at P&G.

He faced a challenge that would have tested the most experienced CEO. P&G needed nothing less than a radical overhaul of its entire approach to innovation. His predecessor saw P&G as first and foremost a research and development company, and spent accordingly. Only heavy investment in research and development, he maintained, would reignite sales and drive growth. In his eighteen-month tenure as CEO, he tripled innovation spending.

Whatever the merits of that theory, it yielded disappointing results in practice. Only 15 percent of innovation projects met internal sales and profit targets. Give it time, said the theory's defenders. The strategy will work, but it will take more than a quarter or two.

Other senior executives saw P&G as primarily a marketing and brand-building enterprise. The company, they said, should focus on brands and marketing and allow R&D spending to drift back down to its historical level. That was the P&G way, said those executives, and it had worked just fine until Lafley's predecessor tampered with it.

Reconciling the Irreconcilable

Lafley entered the CEO's office, then, under pressure to opt for one of two sharply opposed models. Both sides argued that their model was, in fact, reality—"the way things are." Lafley didn't see it that way. He treated the opposing models as hypotheses rather than the truth, which gave him the intellectual and emotional latitude to weigh the merits and drawbacks of both models without needing to defend one and declare the other false.

From his disinterested vantage point, Lafley was able to see that returning to historical levels of R&D spending was not going to produce the growth P&G needed. The market had changed. P&G was surrounded by fierce competitors, including store brands and private-label products that were eating into P&G's market share. The company needed to counter with innovative new products of its own, which called for a higher level of spending than was customary at P&G.

But Lafley could also see that the sharply increased innovation spending his predecessor favored wasn't the entire answer either. Yes, there were some promising new products on the drawing board, but the company simply couldn't afford to wait to see if the promised return on its massive R&D investment would materialize.

Lafley set his sights on a resolution that would be superior to either existing alternative. He had no intention of settling for half measures. Like an artist, Lafley considered a piece of work unacceptable until it reached a certain quality standard, and an option with unpleasant trade-offs was not going to meet that standard.

Lafley also took personal responsibility for his dilemma. Rather than blame the world at large for presenting him with a difficult choice, Lafley assumed the real problem lay within himself. "I haven't yet," he said to himself, "found a creative resolution that meets my standards. That's not the world's fault. I just haven't thought hard enough yet."

Lafley took a step back and began to question assumptions that other P&G executives had taken for granted. He questioned the causal reasoning that said useful innovation output is directly proportional to the dollars invested in it. He asked himself if there were other, better ways to produce innovations than to pour money into P&G's own research and development labs. He looked outside P&G to see how other organizations solved their innovation problems.

He discovered that innovation was broadly distributed. Solo inventors, academics, and small companies were disproportionately represented, while big corporations had a lower share than would be expected, given their size and resources. But big corporations, with manufacturing, marketing, and distribution capabilities far beyond the reach of the small players, did have an advantage in developing, testing, and commercializing breakthrough ideas.

Free of preconceptions about the "right" way to innovate, Lafley saw a way to hitch small-company inventiveness to P&G's vast network of resources. He set a target for P&G to obtain 50 percent of its innovations from outside the company by connecting with a wide array of outside innovators. P&G would then exploit its huge resource advantage to develop and commercialize the innovation. Lafley believed this strategy, dubbed "Connect & Develop," would enable P&G to parlay a relatively modest investment in innovation into above-average growth.

P&G's research and development staff greeted Lafley's proposed resolution with consternation. "I had principal scientists—PhDs—angry because they thought that we were going to outsource," Lafley said. "They thought that we were walking away from innovation, which was the lifeblood of the company. I said no, *au contraire*, what we are really trying to do is double or triple the productivity of the R&D labs; we want to get more of this stuff commercialized."[6]

One of the first fruits of the Connect & Develop initiative was the Spinbrush, a low-priced, battery-powered oscillating toothbrush. P&G acquired it early in its commercialization from a tiny company that based it on the Spin-pop, a battery-powered spinning lollipop that was wildly popular among prepubescents. P&G's contribution was to slap the Crest brand—a beloved and venerable brand name in oral care—on it and distribute it to stores across the country. The combination was irresistible. Within four years, this connection of P&G's marketing and distribution muscle with small-enterprise innovation developed into a $160 million product line.[7]

Lafley didn't do it alone. He would be the first to give P&G's top innovation executives—Gil Cloyd, Larry Huston, and Nabil Sakkab—credit for formulating and executing Connect & Develop.[8] But they wouldn't have brought the idea to fulfillment without Lafley's ability to distinguish between reality and models of reality, his unyielding high standards, his assumption of personal responsibility, and his willingness—eagerness, really—to rethink the entire problem from the ground up. Lafley created a leadership environment that encouraged Cloyd, Huston, and Sakkab to push their idea as far as it would go. Lafley then used his credibility and organizational authority to put the idea into operation. Integrative thinking should not be confused with solo, heroic leadership. But it is leadership all the same.

How Red Hat Found Profits in Free Software

One of the most fascinating stories in the entire technology sector has been the rising challenge by Linux, the open-source operating system, to Microsoft's once-monopolistic dominance of the market for operating system software. Richard Stallman, the MIT professor who put forth the theory of "open-source" software development, and Finnish engineer Linus Torvalds, who developed the foundational code, or kernel, of Linux, are clearly the two most important figures in this story. The next most important person may be Bob Young, cofounder of Red Hat software, the dominant Linux distributor. Young's creative resolution of a crucial strategic dilemma was the event that put Red Hat—and Linux—on the path to profit and power in the marketplace.

Young stands out, even in an industry full of eccentrics. Slight and balding, always sporting red socks and a red hat, he's given to almost feverish disquisitions about the industry he loves. He insists he's not "one of the smart guys" in his industry, but he has changed it profoundly.[9]

To understand how, a little history is in order. In the 1980s, a movement had taken shape, spurred by Richard Stallman's theorizing, to develop software based on UNIX, an operating system invented in the 1970s at AT&T Bell Labs and made available at no cost to anyone who requested a copy.

Torvalds was one of thousands of programmers and enthusiasts who obtained a copy of UNIX and started tinkering with it. In 1991, he posted a message on a UNIX users' bulletin board, modestly announcing that he'd developed an operating system from the UNIX kernel and offering his fellow enthusiasts a look. Before long, suggested improvements to Torvalds' program, dubbed Linux, were pouring in. To capture the improvements and integrate them into the program, Torvalds and a few colleagues set up a loosely organized committee to vet all the suggestions and incorporate the most meritorious into the core program.

By 1993, Linux had evolved to the point where it was robust enough to handle heavy-duty corporate applications. But corporations weren't buying because the market was fragmented and confusing, with many competing versions of the uncopyrighted software floating around cyberspace. Enterprises like Yggdrasil and Slackware Linux tried to bring some order to the chaos, selling their own versions of Linux to interested buyers. Young ran an outfit called ACC Corp. that distributed their "free software."

The term was something of a misnomer. Linux was actually just extremely cheap. Purchasers would pay a small fee for a CD-ROM of the software, either directly from a developer like Yggdrasil or Slackware or from a distributor such as ACC. But unlike conventional companies such as Microsoft, Linux vendors didn't charge a license fee scaled to the number of users of the operating system.

Instead, Linux purchasers were free to mount their system on as many computers as they wished, at no additional cost.

One of the companies that sold its version of Linux through ACC was an operation called Red Hat Linux. Impressed by the product, Young combined his company with Red Hat, becoming CEO of what was now called Red Hat Software and shifting the company's focus from distribution of several flavors of Linux to direct sales of Red Hat's Linux product.

From his experience as a distributor, Young knew that the still-tiny market for Linux software was growing rapidly. But the business was going to hit a ceiling unless it could find a new business model.

Young could see that the two dominant models then in existence were profoundly flawed. On one hand, there was the classical proprietary software model the big players such as Microsoft and Oracle employed. They sold their clients only the operating software, not the source code. All enhancements and modifications were in the hands of the software maker. As Young likes to say: "Buying proprietary software is like buying a car with the hood welded shut. If something goes wrong, you are not able to even try to fix it."

The providers sold their proprietary product at a high price—for example, $209 for Microsoft's important release of that period, Windows 95, with gross margins above 90 percent—serviced it at a high price, and released regular upgrades that customers had to buy if they wanted to capture the software company's incremental improvements.

Young has nothing but scorn for this way of doing business. "If you ran into a bug that caused your systems to crash," he says, "you would call up the manufacturer and say, 'My systems are crashing.' And he'd say, 'Oh, dear.' What he really meant was, 'Oh, good.' He'd send an engineer over at several hundred dollars an hour to fix his software for you that was broken when he delivered it to you, and he called this customer service." In opposition to this problematic way of doing business was the free software model employed by Slackware, Yggdrasil, and Red Hat itself.

Young didn't think either model had much of a future. The proprietary software model, in his view, was an inefficient and obsolescent way to develop software. But the "free software" model was problematic as well. "You couldn't make any money selling [the Linux] operating system," Young says, "because all this stuff was free, and if you started to charge money for it, someone else would come in and price it lower. It was a commodity in the truest sense of the word."

If Red Hat was going to be something more than a low-margin distributor of a commodity product, it would have to find some way of adding value to Linux that didn't involve improving the code. That meant finding something salient about the Linux business that other programmers and distributors had overlooked.

Young found that point of salience in corporate buying habits. Young realized that because big companies are making decisions that they will have to live with for ten or even twenty years, they want to buy from the industry leader. "If Merrill Lynch was going to choose someone to support their use of Linux," Young says, "they weren't going to choose the number-two Linux developer. They were going to choose the number-one."

Proceeding from that insight, Young discovered a causal relationship between sales level and sustainability that his rivals had overlooked. "If we were the number-two brand, we did not have a business of any value whatsoever. If you're going to sell free software, you'd better be the number-one player at it if you hope to get any leverage in the marketplace."

How, then, could Red Hat establish itself as the Linux market leader in the eyes of corporate users? By imposing order and control on the chaotic process by which improvements to Linux are developed and captured. But let Young explain it himself:

> *A typical Linux operating system, whether Red Hat or Slackware, is some 800 to 1,000 different packages all compiled together. Those packages are maintained by different teams of people, and those people update those packages once or twice a year. If you accept, for argument's sake, that they get updated once a year, that's closing in on three updates a day. You, as a systems administrator for Merrill Lynch, have to keep track of all those updates and deploy them across all of your Linux servers if you're going to use Linux.*
>
> *If you use Microsoft, you don't have that problem. Microsoft delivers you a new version once every six months and they tell you how to install it. You have this nice, safe, controlled deployment of your new software.*
>
> *You can see that serious corporate users weren't going to use [Linux]. Although the price was right, they wouldn't save money if they used free software where their systems administrators had to track all of the random updates.*

But they would save money—and have a more stable, reliable operating system than Windows—if there were a way to manage the flood of updates. Red Hat would make itself invaluable to customers by taking on that management task.

Young was pleased with this resolution, which blended the best elements of the two competing business models into a new way of doing business. But there was a hitch. A big one. Corporate customers wouldn't buy Red Hat's Linux unless Red Hat was the clear leader in the Linux space.

Red Hat would have to find its way onto every hard drive in corporate America. To get there, Young's programming team rewrote the Red Hat version of Linux so that it could be distributed over the Internet instead of via CD-ROM. Then Young told his team, "We're going to put it up on every FTP [File Transfer Protocol] server we can find on the Internet everywhere in the world, and we are going to encourage people to download it for free."

Young's goal was, he says, "to give [Linux] away more efficiently" than any of his competitors. It was a risky move. Red Hat was sacrificing all the potential revenue it stood to earn from its new release of Linux. But that was the price of making Red Hat's version of Linux the de facto standard. In a stroke, Red Hat's Linux became legitimate in the eyes of the corporate users.

In 1999, Red Hat went public, and Young became a billionaire in the first day of trading. By 2000, Linux had captured 25 percent of the server operating system market, and Red Hat held over 50 percent of the global market for Linux systems. And unlike the vast majority of the dot-com era's start-ups, Red Hat has continued to grow.

What made the creative resolution of Red Hat possible? Young treated the existence of unattractive alternative models exactly as we would expect an integrative thinker to do. He recognized that the existing proprietary software and free software models weren't reality; they were simply the accepted models for coping with dynamics of the software business. Second, he didn't rest until he found a new business model that was clearly better than the existing alternatives. Third, he took personal responsibility for figuring out a new way to compete, instead of accepting the choices offered him. Fourth, he read the existence of unpleasant trade-offs as a signal to rethink the problem from the ground up. In doing so, he found clues to what was salient to corporate software buyers and gained a key insight into the causal relationship between industry leadership and prosperity. His path to a creative resolution was remarkably similar in its structure to the paths forged by Sharp and Lafley.

The Buzz Machine That Ate Toronto

Piers Handling fits the role of film festival director to a tee. He has lived in the world of film from a young age, and it's a world he tears himself away from only reluctantly. At gala parties, he appears to be wishing he was watching yet another of the festival's most obscure films rather than mingling with the stars. But he is more than an afficionado of the art of film. He is also a keen student of the business of film.

When Handling joined the staff of the Toronto International Film Festival (TIFF) in 1982, the festival was the very model of a struggling start-up.[10] Launched in 1976, it was barely international and in its own country it trailed the Montreal World Film Festival in prominence and prestige.

It was still a second-tier festival at best when Handling was appointed the festival's director in 1994, after stints as program director and artistic director. Handling's board wanted the Toronto festival to draw the same sort of excited notice enjoyed by the top European festivals in Venice, New York, Berlin, and Cannes. The ticket to the big leagues, board members believed, were the jury prizes the top festivals awarded. Cannes had the famed Palme d'Or—how could the TIFF top that?

Juried festivals were one of the festival world's two dominant models. Panels composed of industry luminaries—directors, producers, actors—would award prizes to a festival's outstanding films, ensuring them prestige and, usually, wide distribution (the Palme d'Or awarded to Michael Moore's *Fahrenheit 9/11*, for example, was instrumental to that film's box-office success around the world). The major benefit of the juried model was the media buzz and attention that accrued to prize-winning films.

But the jury was by its nature elitist, creating a gap between the festival-goers and the festival itself. Handling believed that the presence of an elite jury made it difficult for the people who paid the festival's bills with their ticket purchases to feel that the festival was truly theirs.

Non-juried festivals eliminated the element of elitism and gave the movie-lovers who attended a sense of ownership. But in the absence of prizes, a festival and its films had no easy way to capture the news media's attention and generate buzz. And buzz was what the TIFF board desperately desired.

Like Sharp, Lafley, and Young, then, Handling faced two less-than-ideal options. Salient to him was the TIFF's grassroots atmosphere. "Toronto was designed to be inclusive, designed to be populist, designed to be for an audience, not designed to be a festival for experts," he told me. But the needs of film producers and film distributors were also salient to him. Film producers wanted big crowds to create the buzz that would draw film distributors. And film distributors looked to festivals for signals of what would draw crowds in their own markets.

What every player in the equation needed was buzz. The festival itself needed buzz to attract an audience; the producers needed buzz to sell their movies; and the distributors needed buzz to judge which movies to buy.

Buzz fed on itself in a virtuous circle. If a festival generated buzz, more movie stars would show up. Their presence would feed the media's buzz machine, and that in turn would bring in more moviegoers, producers, and distributors. There was no buzz without a prize, but a prize itself, with its negative overtones of elitism, could kill the very buzz it was supposed to generate.

Handling understood these complex causal relationships and also appreciated how each piece linked to the other. As he thought through this complex causal map, a creative resolution began to take shape. TIFF's continued growth required a buzz-generating prize to continue into the global elite. But that prize had to excite and involve moviegoers rather than make them feel left out.

The resolution was right under Handling's nose. Although the TIFF was not a juried festival, it had, since 1978, awarded a prize to the festival's most popular film. But the People's Choice Award, which the festival's filmgoers themselves voted on, got little attention from the press, festival-goers, or TIFF management. Handling realized that with the right promotion, the People's Choice Award could become a buzz-generating vehicle that was truly populist in nature, transforming a traditionally elitist activity into something that belonged to every movie lover who attended the festival.

By making the audience itself the jury, the festival would give paying customers a powerful incentive to see as many movies as possible. The competition would satisfy the media's desire for a horse race, ensuring plenty of coverage. And the TIFF People's Choice Award would give distributors a clear signal of a movie's likely commercial appeal. The directors might prefer a juried prize awarded by their peers, but they'd settle for popular acclaim without undue complaint.

The People's Choice Award put the Toronto International Film Festival on the map. By 1999, Roger Ebert, America's most influential film critic, was telling one reporter that "although Cannes is still larger, Toronto is more useful and more important."[11] By 2005, TIFF had booked the largest volume of sales in film festival history, and film critic Liam Lacey named it "the most important film festival in the world—the largest, the most influential, the most inclusive."[12]

As the *Hollywood Reporter* said in 2005, "The Toronto International Film Festival increasingly has become the premier launching pad for studios looking to unveil their award-season hopefuls."[13] Winners of the People's Choice Award include *Shine*, which won an Oscar in 1996; *Life Is Beautiful*, which took three Oscars in 1998; *American Beauty*, winner of five Oscars in 1999; *Crouching Tiger, Hidden Dragon*, which captured four Oscars in 2000; *Whale Rider*, nominated for one Oscar in 2002; *Hotel Rwanda*, nominated for three Oscars in 2004; and *Tsotsi*, which won one Oscar in 2005.

And it all started with the People's Choice Award, a classic product of integrative thinking. In recognizing the award as the key to the Toronto festival's identity and market power, Handling avoided confusing the existing clashing models with reality. He didn't settle for a solution that fell short of his own standards. He took personal responsibility for a creative resolution. And when he encountered unpleasant trade-offs, he revisited his thinking to search for a creative resolution. The one he found reinforced TIFF's position as a populist film festival that respected audiences as well as the commercial and artistic needs of the film community.

Common Paths to Unique Solutions

In forging creative resolutions to the unpleasant trade-offs they faced, Lafley, Young, and Handling illustrate the patterns common to the many integrative thinkers I have studied. Like the other integrative thinkers, the three leaders were able to separate models from reality. They were free to hold the models up to analysis and scrutiny without needing to refute one or the other. This crucial step enabled them to explore the tensions between the opposing models and gather clues pointing toward a better model.

In Lafley's case, the new spending model helped him understand that P&G needed a higher level of innovation to resume growth. The old spending model helped Lafley understand what level of investment P&G could actually afford. In Young's case, the free software model helped him understand the power of broad distribution. The proprietary software model helped him see the potential for earning profits from service. The juried model helped Handling see the value of prize-related buzz. The nonjuried model reminded him of the salience of his audiences' need to feel included.

Like other integrative thinkers, Lafley, Young, and Handling refused to settle for mediocrity and half measures. An unpleasant trade-off signaled to each of them that the current answers simply weren't good enough, even if they appeared to be the only ones available. If an existing model didn't meet their standards, the model would have to change, because the standards wouldn't.

Like other integrative thinkers, Lafley, Young, and Handling took responsibility for finding a satisfactory resolution. Facing nothing but suboptimal solutions, they didn't rail against circumstance; instead, they thought, "I face an unpleasant trade-off because I haven't thought through the problem hard enough, expansively enough, creatively enough." The message they took away when faced with unpleasant choices was not "choose now" but "think harder." And by keeping the whole in mind while working on the individual parts, each was able to find a creative resolution to the tension between the two initial choices.

This drive for the creative resolution of tensions is the single most striking feature of the successful managerial leaders who I interviewed. When I pressed them on why they felt compelled to think past the existing models when everyone around them encouraged them to choose one, I got a few variations on a single answer: "I'm just not an either-or kind of person." Lafley's variant offers the business case for not settling for "or" when "and" is possible. "We weren't going to win if it was an 'or,'" he told me. "Everybody can do 'or;' everybody can do great trade-offs. But you're not going to win if you're in a trade-off game."[14]

CHAPTER 4

Dancing Through Complexity

Shaping Resolutions by Resisting Simplification

Everything should be as simple as possible, but no simpler.

—Albert Einstein

WHEN MARTHA GRAHAM DIED in 1991 at the age of ninety-six, she was a Presidential Medal of Freedom winner, the acknowledged queen of modern dance, and one of *Time* magazine's "100 Greatest Americans of the Twentieth Century."[1] She was also one of the century's most gifted integrative thinkers, whose thought had far-reaching results—so far-reaching it might even be of interest to executives responsible for fashioning creative solutions to perplexing business dilemmas.

Martha Graham joined The Denishawn School dance company of Los Angeles in 1916, following her graduation from the University of Cumnoch in California.[2] It was a time of great artistic ferment. Dance, like painting and literature, was casting off the rigid conventions of the nineteenth century, and a handful of mavericks were pioneering the style that would come to be known as modernism. Graham threw herself into the modern dance movement, and by the early 1920s she was one of its leading lights. When she made her New York debut in 1926, she was already choreographing dances that dispensed with the fluid, prettified line of classical ballet in favor of a "contraction and release" technique characterized by harsh, angular movements. Her dances pulsated with angst and emotion.

Graham's work was utterly contemporary, but the practices of the dance world at the time were still stuck in the nineteenth century. Dances were choreographed to musical scores that for the most part, were not written to accompany a particular dance—most weren't written as dance music at all. The performers wore traditional ballet tunics or folk costumes that bore little connection to the content of the dance. Stage sets were sterile, two-dimensional "flats"—mere backdrops with little or no apparent relation to the dancers or the dance.

That would all change under Martha Graham. Working closely with Lewis Horst, a composer she met at Denishawn, Graham made music integral to the dance it accompanied. She continued that practice throughout her career. For her 1944 masterpiece, *Appalachian Spring*, she collaborated with legendary composer Aaron Copland to create a powerful synergy between music and choreography.

Graham also took a keen interest in costume design, replacing ballet tunics and folk dresses with straight, long shirts and simple leotards. The stage sets for her dances broke the mold as well, by incorporating sculpture and other three-dimensional elements.

Her long and productive collaboration with Isamu Noguchi, the renowned Japanese-America sculptor, resulted in revolutionary stage designs for *Frontier, Appalachian Spring*, and many other dances. Graham's dancers were able to interact with their stage environment, often holding or touching props. This was unprecedented in performance dance.

For Graham, composition, choreography, costumes, and sets were all part of an interdependent, integrated whole. In a sharp break from conventional dance practice, she explicitly considered the whole while working on every element of the production, rather than doling out each element to independent specialists. In doing so, she revolutionized an art form.

Simple Comforts

Theoretically, businesses and their leaders could take a similarly coherent, holistic approach to crafting their products and services. Why don't they? Blame the "factory setting" of the contemporary business organization, which is biased toward simplification and specialization.

And it's not just business organizations. In every domain, human beings gravitate toward simplification and specialization. We do so, says Stanford management theorist Jim March, because we live in a dauntingly complex and ambiguous world, full of causal inconsistencies. We cut prices by 5 percent one month, and sales rise 7 percent. So at the end of the next quarter, we again cut prices 5 percent, but this time sales barely budge. A competitor has introduced a rival offering that has eaten into the anticipated sales gain. Our reaction to this baffling turn of events is to simplify and specialize. "Organizations," he says in an article with colleague Daniel Levinthal, "seek to transform confusing, interactive environments into less confusing, less interactive ones by decomposing domains and treating the resulting sub-domains as autonomous."[3]

We know that we sacrifice something in doing so, rationalizing the sacrifice by referring to what's popularly known as the 80–20 rule. The rule states that for 20 percent of the maximum effort, we can get 80 percent of the ideal result. Applied to the cognitive domain, the rule says that 20 percent of the maximum mental effort will yield 80 percent of the perfect answer. Further, the rule suggests that only an obsessive or pathological perfectionist would invest 80 percent more effort in the hope of reaching an answer that would at best be only 20 percent better.

The 80–20 rule implicitly acknowledges that simplification is not the perfect solution to the problems of ambiguity and causal inconsistency, but rather a coping mechanism. We settle for 80 percent to avoid being overwhelmed by complexity and losing the ability to function at all. When a colleague or superior admonishes us to "quit complicating the issue," it's not just an impatient reminder to get on with the damn job—it's also a plea to keep the complexity at a tolerable level.

As comforting as simplification can be, however, it impairs every step of the integrative thinking process. It encourages us to edit out salient features rather than consider the question of salience broadly. Editing, in turn, leads to unsatisfactory resolutions of the dilemmas that business throws at us. Issy Sharp would not have been able to create the Four Seasons difference if he had simplified as most of his rival hoteliers did. He would not have engaged business travelers in a dialogue deep enough to elicit the crucial information that they longed for their own home and office. That kind of conversation would have raised issues too complex for a specialist-dominated organization to address. But Sharp actually preferred a complicated picture, because he understood, at least implicitly, that simplification, 80–20 style, leads to more business as usual. Truly creative resolutions, Sharp realized, spring from complexity.

Simplification makes us favor linear, unidirectional causal relationships, even if reality is more complex and multidirectional. The simplifying mind would have not grasped Handling's causal connection between film festival prizes and the audience's feeling of inclusion, because it is not a straightforward linear relationship.

Simplification also encourages us to construct a limited model of the problem before us, whatever it might be. The alternatives we perceive are meager and unattractive, closing any remaining avenue to an integrative resolution. The simplifying mind has no choice but to settle for trade-offs, also known as the best bad choice available.

Specialization and Its Discontents

Specialization is a variant of simplification. If the simplifying mind attempts to understand the whole picture by making it more shallow and superficial than it really is, the specialist attempts to preserve depth and thoroughness by masking out all but a few square inches of a vast canvas.

Like simplification, specialization allows us to cope with what might be overwhelming complexity. Consider medicine, by any measure a massively complex field. The medical field copes by mandating intensive and formalized specialization. There are official specialties, such as obstetrics and gynecology, and subspecialties, such as neonatology. Subspecialists possess a staggering depth of knowledge of their corner of the medical universe but only a thin layer of knowledge about medicine outside their subspecialty. Subspecialists also tend to take little interest in or responsibility for developments outside their subspecialties.

At its best, medicine weaves the deep knowledge of each specialty and subspecialty into a seamless fabric of patient care. But at its all-too-frequent worst, specialized medicine cares for discrete parts of the body without ever recognizing the whole person standing before it. Think back to your last visit to a hospital. You likely interacted with several specialists, and they probably didn't spend much time sharing their particular perspectives on your case with their fellow physicians. Chances are you checked out of the hospital feeling that your heart, knees, and sinuses (for instance) had been subjected to microscopic scrutiny, but that no one stepped back to consider you as a whole person. You may also have felt dissatisfied, even resentful. Dissatisfaction with the dehumanizing consequences of conventional medicine's specialization has spurred the emergence of the alternative medicine movement.

The business world has proceeded down a similar path of specialization, with equally unsatisfactory results. Business's dominant mode of specialization is the functional area—finance, marketing, production, sales, human resources, and the rest of the organizational chart. Each functional area has its own accepted range of salience, its own accepted causal relationships, its own training, its own insiders' language, and its own culture.

As in medicine, specialization in business enables practitioners to accumulate deep knowledge. With time and effort, managers can acquire encyclopedic expertise in finance, marketing, or accounting. But that expertise actually works against the development of expertise in business itself. As Peter Drucker told me, "The business that is going to hire your new MBA will hire somebody to do specialized work. And for the first five, eight, ten years, your students will work as specialists. And in most organizations, it is resented if they show any interest in anything but their specialties. They're then pushy, or nosy, or empire builders."[4] But specialists aren't optimally suited to solve the biggest problems businesses face, because as Drucker also pointed out, "there are no finance decisions, tax decisions, or marketing decisions; only business decisions."

Functional specialization is especially inimical to integrative thinking because it undermines productive architecture—the keeping in mind of the whole while working on the individual parts. Functional specialization encourages the sequential or parallel resolution of discrete parts of a business problem. The result is that what is optimal from the perspective of one function will take precedence over what is optimal for the firm as a whole.

When designing a new product, for instance, the research and development department arrives at a formula and a set of specifications. Then R&D "throws over the wall"—an expression that speaks volumes about the balkanization of most complex business organizations—to manufacturing, which in turn throws it over the wall to marketing, and then to sales, and so on. Each subsequent function is saddled with the narrowly provincial decisions of the previous functions in the chain. So if R&D specialists didn't consider manufacturability when they designed the product, the manufacturing function will just have to do the best it can. The next step down the line can expect similar disregard for its priorities.

The usual alternative to the sequential process is a parallel process in which the general manager of a project asks each functional unit to produce a solution to a common problem. Again, because of the degree of skill specialization, the people in each functional unit lack the range to consider features of the problem that might be salient to specialists in other functions. Nor can one specialist see the causal relationships that other specialists might see.

As a result, each function is likely to come back to the general manager with its own functional optimum, none of which is likely to embody all the features of a firm optimum. The general manager must then either pick one functional option or try to piece together a sort of Frankenstein's monster from parts of each solution. The result is often something like Pontiac's ill-fated Aztec SUV. The car was supposed to be the product of the best ideas of Pontiac's engineers, marketers, and customers. But because there was no integrating intelligence drawing all those good ideas into a unified whole, the Aztec looked like what it was: a hodgepodge of good ideas that had never been integrated into single good design. The Aztec is no longer on the market.

Neither the sequential nor the parallel process generates the productive architecture characteristic of integrative thinking, in which the thinker keeps the whole in mind while working on the individual parts. So why, then, do we simplify and specialize, even knowing it produces results that are less than optimal? "The reason that the world is cut into little pieces is because it is easier to deal with," explains Hilary Austen Johnson, who studied under Jim March. "Once you start integrating things, you end up with a much more complex problem than you had before. It's harder to work with. Things are more in flux. You get more interactions between things, so the knowledge that you have has to be more robust."[5]

That's more complexity than most minds care to handle, and simplification and specialization can quickly come to look like the only refuge from chaos. But experienced integrative thinkers learn to draw a distinction between chaos and complexity. F. C. Kohli, the founder of Indian software giant Tata Consultancy Services and the man often called the father of the Indian software industry, offers encouragement to anyone facing a complex problem:

> *Any situation has a certain number of alternatives, but if you are doing system thinking, even for a complex problem, and you realize what is the system, what are the subsystems, what are the sub-subsystems, and you define their interrelationship as well as you can, you will start seeing some daylight, how to get out of it. The complexity—if you have some logical inputs and also have a system structure—I don't think it looks that bad.*[6]

In other words, complexity doesn't have to be overwhelming, if we can master our initial panic reaction and look for patterns, connections, and causal relationships. Our capacity to handle complexity, Kohli suggests, is greater than we give ourselves credit for.

Teams can offer valuable support in maintaining the complexity that integrative thinking thrives upon. Martha Graham collaborated with giants from the domains of music and art such as Copland and Noguchi because she valued and needed their expertise. They helped her break free from conventional notions of what was salient to the dance and deepened her understanding of causal relationships among each element of the performance. Constant interaction with collaborators helped her keep the whole dance in mind as she designed its individual elements. In such an environment, a creative resolution isn't assured, but the odds of success are dramatically improved.

Like Graham, the integrative thinkers I interviewed knew they would need plenty of help to reach creative resolutions. They chose their collaborators expressly for what they could contribute to an integrated whole. Bruce Mau, a renowned designer and frequent collaborator with architect Frank Gehry, told me, "You can't make a renaissance person anymore, because the range of what you would need to do is just impossible. But you could actually assemble a renaissance team."[7] The integrative thinkers rely on their "renaissance teams" to broaden salience, maintain sophisticated causality, and create a holistic architecture in their drive for creative resolution.

Designing a Ride, Not a Railcar

One of the most sophisticated and successful renaissance teams in business today is the industrial design firm IDEO. What gives IDEO its edge is that CEO Tim Brown and his colleagues recognize that the people who use products and services don't judge them simply by their functional performance. They also judge them by the degree of emotional satisfaction they provide. How a kitchen utensil makes its user feel is as important as how it chops or cuts. Many of IDEO's competitors have belatedly come to the same realization, but IDEO got there first, and it has much more experience than its rivals in designing for the emotions, for the heart as well as the hand.[8]

Brown explicitly discourages both his designers and IDEO's clients from oversimplifying and overspecializing. Excessive focus on the individual elements of a design problem, he argues, will detract from the overall solution that clients are seeking.

That belief was put to the test a few years back, when Amtrak, the U.S. passenger rail corporation, was preparing to launch its Acela high-speed train service along the Boston-to-Washington metropolitan corridor. It asked IDEO to design the interior of its Acela rail coaches. Amtrak wanted a railcar that was more attractive and functional than the interior of the passenger airliners that were Amtrak's primary competition.

Brown could have taken on the assignment and designed a car that would have been a huge improvement over Amtrak's dowdy and rundown rolling stock. But Brown is an integrative thinker who rejects simplification and specialization. He argued that Amtrak, by focusing on the interior of its cars, was missing a much larger problem. Travelers didn't favor the airlines over Amtrak because they disliked Amtrak's cars. Travelers avoided Amtrak because they disliked the entire Amtrak experience. They didn't like booking tickets on Amtrak, they didn't like waiting in Amtrak stations, they didn't like the boarding procedures. Once they'd run that gauntlet, Amtrak's cars could have been furnished in silk and gold, and it wouldn't have made a difference.

Brown persuaded Amtrak to rethink the design challenge and put IDEO's designers to work analyzing the typical train trip. They determined it involved ten distinct steps: learning, planning, starting, entering, ticketing, waiting, boarding, riding, arriving, and continuing (their subsequent journey). The interior of the railcar was relevant to only one of ten steps in the customer experience: riding.

Brown describes his work for Amtrak and IDEO's other clients as "a synthetic process" that takes into account "the whole thing, whatever that thing is." In Amtrak's case, "the whole thing" involved an end-to-end rethink of the entire Acela customer experience—

the very definition of holistic architecture. Not only were Acela railcars redesigned, so were train stations, interactive information kiosks, employee workstations, and indeed the Acela brand, which was positioned as an experience that was superior in every respect to air travel.

The Acela is a shining example of the breakthroughs possible when simplification and specialization are set aside in favor of viewing both problem and solution in all their complexity. Now let's meet another integrative thinker who also chose to wrestle with the individual components of a business problem without ever forgetting that they were parts of a greater whole.

Moses Znaimer: Local Hero, Global Conquest

Moses Znaimer is a compact and animated man who has lived and breathed television ever since he bought a television set with money from his bar mitzvah in the mid-1950s. In 1972, Znaimer cofounded Citytv, an independent Toronto television station that competed against two giant Canadian networks, government-owned CBC and private CTV, as well as the Buffalo affiliates of the three big American networks of the day, CBS, NBC, and ABC.[9]

It was a challenging environment, but Znaimer's quirky little station managed to thrive by making a virtue of necessity. Where mainstream TV was polished, practiced, and bland, Citytv was funky, spontaneous, and idiosyncratic. It featured hip newscasters, fringe U.S. and European shows, and, late at night, movies that were racier than anything the big competitors would dare to show at any hour.

But mere survival wasn't enough for Znaimer. By the early 1980s, it was clear to him that the competitive landscape was changing, requiring him to make a significant choice. On the one hand, the broadcast media business was globalizing. CNN and MTV were emerging as global brands and operations, and other regional media powerhouses, such as BSkyB in Europe and Rupert Murdoch's News Corporation empire in Asia, weren't far behind. The global players, he realized, could move into individual local markets brandishing resources that local players had no hope of matching.

On the other hand, he saw that viewers still loved their local television stations, which connected with communities in a way that the global players, cable channels, and superstations could not. Advertisers were eager to reach those local viewers, and their continued spending gave the local stations a solid economic underpinning, even as the global behemoths grew larger and more powerful.

The apparent choice that Znaimer faced was to stay local or go global. If Citytv stayed local, it risked being swamped as the TV business globalized. It was already happening in other industries. From retailing to consumer packaged goods to movies, Znaimer could see that players with global scale were beating the locals.

But the global alternative was equally unsatisfactory. Going global meant taking on huge financial risk. Citytv would have to borrow huge sums of capital, make expensive acquisitions with no guarantee that they'd earn out, and find the management talent to negotiate tricky alliances while expanding at breakneck speed. Even if everything broke Citytv's way, it might not catch the global players, who had a head start of a decade or more.

Znaimer's easiest choice would have been to stay comfortably local, in the belief that going global was beyond his reach. The big players would swallow him up eventually, but he'd make a good living while waiting for the end. That's what a conventional thinker would likely have done. When facing any dilemma with nasty trade-offs on both sides, the conventional thinker declares there is really no choice at all.

But being an integrative thinker, Znaimer refused to accept the slow encroachment of international media players into his market, just as he refused to miss out on the globalization of media. He rethought the question of global versus local, looking for salient information he overlooked the first time.

He found it. The love of local media, he realized, wasn't limited to Toronto. Viewers in almost every local market are powerfully attached to the homegrown stations that reflect and foster the community's values and sense of itself as a community. Local media, Znaimer told me, helps members of a community find "unexpected connections." That may sound obvious, but Znaimer, unlike his rivals, integrated his insight into Citytv's operating philosophy. As Znaimer explains—in terms that might be a working definition of salience—a key to his station's success is that "at City, we pay attention to things that others have chosen to ignore."

In Znaimer's view, stations have, or at least could have, distinct identities, separate and apart from the programming they carried. "Many would say, 'People don't watch stations, they watch programs,'" he told me. "But that's because most stations aren't there. Stations can speak through everything they produce themselves, through the space between the programs. I believe that the character is in the delivery."

Znaimer uses "the space between the programs"—which other TV executives consider dead air—to create Citytv's distinct identity. The station's personalities appear between programs to tell viewers what's coming next and why they should stick around. Those personalities reflect Toronto's ethnic diversity better than any competitor or any foreign station, creating another bond with the audience. And with their regular, rhythmic appearances in the spaces between shows, they embody Znaimer's dictum that "the nature of TV is flow, not show."

From the start, Znaimer used simple-seeming, mutually reinforcing devices to forge a distinctive identity for Citytv, starting with its tagline: "Citytv—Everywhere . . ." Citytv, the line implies, is connected to every part of the city; it's anywhere anything interesting is happening. Reinforcing that notion is Citytv's fleet of television trucks, which are ubiquitous in Toronto. They carry Citytv's "videographers"—the camera-toting correspondents whose interactions with passersby are broadcast throughout the day as a sort of running commentary on the world.

These rather simple devices create a bond between Citytv and its audience that national and global outlets can't hope to replicate. So does the feature known as "Speaker's Corner." Speaker's Corner is tiny studio booth in Citytv's headquarters building, accessible from the street. Anyone passing by can step in to the booth and film a fifteen-second message. If the message is interesting or thoughtful or funny or touching enough, it will be broadcast in "the space between the programs."

Citytv's real estate also reinforces its connection with its viewers. The Citytv building is located on Queen Street West, Toronto's equivalent of Times Square, and gives the area much of its identity. The station's first-floor studios open up to the street, and its mammoth internal courtyard is the site of numerous parties and entertainment features. The big U.S. networks now all have ground-floor studios in Manhattan that interact with the local street life. They're copying Znaimer, who was the first to make his station's connection with its local environment the cornerstone of its identity.

If Znaimer's identity-creating devices are simple, his view of the causal relationships in the TV business is anything but. In the 1980s, most of his counterparts assumed globalization would eventually erode the attachment to local stations. But Znaimer realized that globalization would actually increase viewers' appetite for TV with a local flavor. Or as he puts it, "globalization drives localization." The more connected viewers feel to their local station, the more they will stick with it when invited to switch to one of the myriad of alternatives. But Znaimer also recognized that global players have the resources and economies of scale that allow them to invest in things a local player couldn't afford.

Like other integrative thinkers, Znaimer describes himself, without any prodding, as "not an 'either-or' kind of guy but rather a 'both-and' guy." So he was never likely to accept a view of the TV business as simply a matter of globalization versus localization, with unsatisfactory trade-offs in both directions. Instead, he has squared the circle by making Citytv the template for quintessentially local television stations across the world. In his words, he has "globalized the science of local television."

Citytv is now a truly global enterprise with affiliated stations in twenty-two countries around the world. In more than 100 countries, local stations unaffiliated to Citytv license its content and style of presentation. That licensing revenue provides Citytv with a resource base that's not available to purely local players, allowing it to compete with the global players without losing its local advantage.

"Glocalization," as Znaimer calls it, is his creative resolution of the tension inherent in the television business. In the classic manner of integrative thinkers, Znaimer fashioned a creative resolution out of apparently irreconcilable alternatives by separating existing models from reality, setting unyielding standards, and taking responsibility instead of claiming to be a victim of circumstance. His view of what was salient was broader than that of the conventional thinkers around him, and he explored more sophisticated causal relationships among the salient elements. He kept the whole firmly in mind while he worked on the parts, and he drove relentlessly for a creative resolution. In doing so, he demonstrates both how integrative thinkers think and why integrative thinking is worth the trouble.

CHAPTER 5

Mapping the Mind

How Thought Circulates

By three methods we may learn wisdom: first, by reflection,
which is noblest; second, by imitation, which is easiest; and
third by experience, which is the bitterest.

—Confucius

IN THE FIRST HALF OF THIS BOOK, we observed integrative thinkers using their opposable minds to produce strikingly positive outcomes. We watched Issy Sharp build a world-standard hotel chain by taking a wide view of what might be salient to his business problem. We saw Bob Young discover unexpected causal relationships that unlocked the door to market leadership for Red Hat. And we saw Moses Znaimer keep his television station's programming, community presence, and competitive context in mind as he devised the architecture of a unique solution to the problem of local media in a global era.

In considering salience, causality, and architecture, the integrative thinkers we studied didn't retreat into simplification and specialization. They waded into untidiness and complexity, confident they'd find an elegant resolution in the end. Like A. G. Lafley considering how to advance Procter & Gamble's innovation agenda, integrative thinkers recognize that unsatisfactory options aren't reality but only a model of reality built up from conscious and unconscious inferences. When presented with multiple unsatisfactory options, Michael Lee-Chin and other integrative thinkers don't take the easy way out and pick the least-worst alternative; they view the creation of a truly attractive option as both their goal and their personal responsibility. They learn from each option without being bound by its limitations, and they use the insights gained to break through to an entirely new model that creatively resolves the tensions between existing models.

I'm now going to shift the focus to developing your opposable mind and building your integrative thinking capacity. To illustrate key concepts, I'll refer to the integrative thinkers I've interviewed, as well as materials and techniques that my colleagues and I have used to teach integrative thinking to MBA students and executives. In the present chapter, we'll set the stage for the final three chapters by mapping a model for your own personal knowledge system. The tripod supporting the system is what I call your stance, tools, and experiences. In the chapters that follow, we take a closer look at each in turn. We examine how to apply specific integrative thinking skills to each component of your personal knowledge system, and observe how exemplary integrative thinkers applied their skills. And we look at how to bring your stance, tools, and experiences to bear on the toughest business problems, the ones that seem to have no good answer.[1]

To get acquainted with the concepts of stance, tools, and experience, let's return to Bob Young, the cofounder and former CEO of Red Hat (he handed off CEO duties to Matthew Szulik in 1999; he's now busy with Lulu.com, an online self-publishing service). In the fall of 2003, Young sat down with me at the Rotman School in Toronto, in front of an audience of business school students and faculty. Over the course of seven ninety-minute sessions, the mercurial and self-deprecating billionaire talked about, well, almost everything: his penchant for wearing pajamas while running a start-up out of what was supposed to be his wife's sewing room; what it was like to run a business next to a worm factory; why he bought a bankrupt professional football team in his home town of Hamilton; and his passion for protecting what's left of the endangered public domain. Most of all, Young told us how he thinks. Better yet, he showed us.[2]

Stance: Who You Are and What You're After

At the top of your personal knowledge food chain is your stance. It is your most broad-based knowledge domain in which you define who you are in your world and what you are trying to accomplish in it. Stance is how you see the world around you, but it's also how you see yourself in that world.

Young sees the world as a complicated place with an almost infinite number of branching paths to follow. "There is always more than one way to succeed in any given situation," he says. But success rarely comes at the first attempt. "Whatever we adopt as our first answer," he says, "is bound to be wrong." Among the most vexing complications in this world are the other people in it, such as customers. "Customers are not always right . . . Customers lie or they are wrong." It's a world where the smartest people don't always have the best ideas. At Red Hat, he worked with what he calls "the smart guys, all the guys with serious top-heavy IQ. None of them were business guys, so they didn't know what the correct answer was."

If the world's problems are so complex that they defeat even the smart guys, it's no wonder there are so many mediocre organizations. They're the norm, in fact, and the sooner people in business admit that, the sooner their organizations can improve. "Don't think you're any good," he told the audience at the Rotman School. "And don't get defensive about it. It's not something to be embarrassed by, because the odds are no one else is any good either. That's the big secret. That's what's behind the curtain—no one else is any good."

The world according to Young can be a baffling and intimidating place. The space he occupies within it is not a terribly exalted one, despite the success of Red Hat and all the money he has made. In the early days of the Internet revolution, he says, "most of us were engineers. Most of us were smart guys, unlike me. I was a sales guy." He couldn't bring a towering intellect to the table, he admits in his characteristic self-deprecating style, but he was happy to offer what he had, for whatever it was worth. "My strengths are . . . ," he says, stopping to think. Finally, he comes up with only one: "I'm a good salesman."

Young's humility is an advantage, because it motivates him to learn what he needs to know, and then learn some more. "How do you go," he asks, "from where you start when you first open your doors—where by definition you aren't very good—to being excellent? It's a really interesting and easy secret, which is: just get a little bit better tomorrow. The problem is, when you get to tomorrow, you have to have the same commitment. Just be a little bit better the day after that. That's all it takes, is just this commitment not to be defensive. Don't worry about criticism, because you're not any good, so criticism is always valid."

What would motivate him to make the effort to improve day after day? Money alone isn't enough. What keeps him going is his drive to accomplish something as an actor in this world. "One of my fundamental beliefs is, I want to create value," he says. "It's more important to me to create value than to make money."

Motivation is a vital force in Young's world. When combined with learning, it's a more powerful problem-solving tool than sheer intellect. "You can overcome dumbness through motivation," he says. Patience is also a key virtue, along with a determination not to jump to conclusions. "Wait," he advises, "reserve judgment, and build data over time." Don't act until you've mastered what you need to know to carry out your intention. "I learned early on not to do anything I didn't understand," he says. "It was just one of my core assumptions."

Young engages his world, then, as a motivated and patient learner. By subduing his impulse to go on the defensive and by committing to improving a little bit every day, he can develop a better understanding of a confusing, complex world, in pursuit of his highest goal: to create value for the world.

That is Young's stance. It may be better defined than most, because he's consciously considered it and honed his description of it in forums like the interviews at Rotman. But everyone has a stance, whether they realize it or not, and whether it is explicit or implicit. Everyone's actions emanate from their view of the world and their place in it. Michael Lee-Chin saw the world as an

accepting place that he could to some degree shape to his liking. Early in his career, he developed a view of himself as a value
investor, and from that view flowed his motivation to build a
renowned investment firm.

Piers Handling's stance was different. He saw himself as a privileged observer in a world full of magnificent films. Too privileged,
in fact: he wanted to give other people the chance to enjoy and
learn from the movies he loved and the new movies he was always
discovering. When he rose to director of the Toronto International Film Festival, he didn't occupy himself solely with managing the festival. He continued to pay close attention to the films
themselves—and why not? His stance originated, after all, in his
view of himself as a lover of movies and their history.

Stance has both individual unique elements and shared cultural
and community aspects. Young saw himself as a member of a community of sales guys who couldn't match the top-heavy IQs of the
smart people, but had accumulated valuable practical experience.
Viewed from another angle, though, the engineers were his com-
rades, fellow soldiers in the army of open-source software revolu-
tionaries. His stance derived in part from his functional association
with the sales guys, and in part from his industry and temporal association with the pioneers of the open-source movement. The
rest of his stance was, and is, as unique as Young himself.

Our stance is often something we take completely for granted.
It is simply "who we are," and we fail to see how our view of who
we are governs our unquestioned assumptions about the "way
things are"—which is to say, our assumptions about the model of
reality that we mistake for reality itself. But even when we take

our stance for granted, it guides us in making sense of the world around us and taking action on the basis of that sense-making. In fact, because we are so often unconscious of our stance and the assumptions about the world that flow from it, its guidance is all the more powerful and all the more difficult to resist or divert.

Tools: Knocking the World into Shape

One step down in your personal knowledge system are the tools you use to organize your thinking and understand your world. Your stance guides what tools you choose to accumulate. Your stance as builder of computers, for instance, will guide you to enroll in a computer engineering program to gain the formal conceptual tools you'll need to design computer hardware.

Tools range from formal theories to established processes to rules of thumb. Young's tool set is entirely devoid of formal theories— not a big surprise, given his view that learning trumps intellect. He doesn't begrudge the top-heavy IQs their fondness for formal theories, but it's hard to miss his implication that they stumble when they try to apply their sophisticated formal theories to the world. He clearly believes they would be better served by a solid grounding in business experience.

So much for the tools Young doesn't use. The ones he does employ derive directly from his stance. The first is his penchant for developing products and services by following a process of prototyping and refining. "I just worked on coming up with strategies that were not incorrect," he says of his years as an entrepreneur, "and then testing them in the marketplace." This tendency follows from his view of himself as a patient learner and the world as a complicated place that no one can figure out perfectly on the first pass.

Young's learning stance leads him to consult widely before making decisions. "When I have talked to the last person," he says, "I have gathered the maximum available information." But because a key element of his stance is his belief that people are much more certain of themselves than they should be, he doesn't necessarily follow the advice he's given, even if it's from a distinguished source. "The smart guys," he says of his decision to distribute Linux over the Internet, "thought it was the stupidest thing."

In addition to these established processes, Young uses rules of thumb, just as we all do. One rule of thumb concerns employee motivation: "It's hard to build a team if people don't like to come to work in the morning." He used that rule of thumb to fire five of the seven subordinates he inherited when he got his first real job. A second rule concerns asset values and the wisdom, or lack thereof, of crowds: "When any asset is dismissed by others, it should be bought." He used that rule of thumb to buy several businesses after leaving Red Hat. A final rule of thumb concerns personal happiness: "Ya gotta do what makes you happy." He used this final rule to quit a high-paying job he hated before having an alternative lined up. At the time, he was living in a house with a big mortgage and his wife was just a month away from the birth of their first child. He knew he had done the right thing shortly after he quit, when the stomach ulcers that had been plaguing him disappeared forever.

Theories, processes, and rules of thumb are efficiency vehicles. Without a conceptual tool kit, you would have to tackle every problem from scratch, proceeding from first principles. Theories, processes, and rules of thumb make it possible to recognize and categorize problems, and apply tools to them that in the past proved effective in similar circumstances. Your browser has crashed often enough for you to recognize that the problem should be solved if you close a few windows and quit the photo program.

As with stance, some of your tools will be yours alone, while others will be community property, as it were. All the investment bankers at Goldman Sachs may share the same models and spreadsheets, and all the derivatives traders across the world may have learned from the same textbook. But through experience, most of them have developed rules of thumb for negotiating acquisitions or assessing risk that are uniquely their own.

Experiences: Where Stance and Tools Meet the World

Your experiences form your most practical and tangible knowledge. The experiences you accumulate are the product of your stance and tools, which guide you toward some experiences and away from others. If your stance as a business executive is as a great model builder and your tools for understanding consumers are sophisticated quantitative models, your experience likely comes from analyzing survey results in your office, not from talking face-to-face with consumers. If instead you see yourself as a people person, skilled at getting consumers to open up about their needs and desires, you will be inclined to build tools for in-home visits and accumulate experiences talking to consumers.

Not surprisingly, Bob Young accumulated a deep and rich body of experience centered around developing and marketing software products. His stance and tools guided him to acquire experience by putting products into the market, gaining feedback from users, improving the product, gaining more feedback, further improving the product, continuing the cycle throughout the product's lifetime. Those experiences are consistent with his stance as a learner whose tools are derived from practical experience rather than formal theories.

Experience enables us to hone our *sensitivities* and *skills*. *Sensitivity* is the capacity to make distinctions between conditions that are similar but not exactly the same. A chef can make fine distinctions between a piece of meat that is done and one that is not quite done. An art critic has the sensitivity to make distinctions between a bold, original talent like Caravaggio, and more timid, conventional craftspeople. An experienced stock analyst can read nearly identical financial statements from two different companies, pinpoint where they diverge, and use experience and rules of thumb to accurately predict which will outperform its peers.

Skill is the capacity to carry out an activity so as to consistently produce the desired result. A skilled chef can consistently cook a steak to the desired state. A skilled art critic can help viewers see the difference between a masterpiece and a merely competent piece of art. A skilled stock analyst can consistently distinguish between stocks that will track the overall market, and those that will outperform it.

Skills and sensitivities tend to grow and deepen in concert. As you repeat a task, you are inclined to build what you learned from the previous repetition into the next iteration, until you develop a consistent technique. An improved technique sharpens your skill, making you faster and more accurate. And as you repeat a task, you learn to make finer and finer distinctions between levels of quality, so that an experienced chef can tell almost by instinct when a steak is bleu, and when it's rare.

When we learn something new, we're acutely aware of features that more experienced practitioners take for granted. Think of your self-consciousness when you learned a new sport or took your first driving lesson. This hyperawareness of yourself and the skill you're learning does not last long. Over time, practice transforms conscious acts into the automatic habits characteristic of mastery. Think of your anxiety at stoplights when you first learned to drive using a standard shift, and the unthinking ease with which you now put the car into first and drive off. The better we get, the faster we forget about what we are doing. Our awareness of what we are doing and how we are accomplishing it quickly becomes as intuitive and inaccessible as the knowledge we use to tie our shoes or ride a bike.

The Dynamics of Your Personal Knowledge System

Personal knowledge develops as a system because its three elements influence one another. Stance guides tool acquisition, which in turn, guides experience accumulation.

The flow, however, is not one-way. Experiences inform the acquisition of more tools. Some tools are shortcuts, where we apply experiential learning to pare away excess effort. In the course of performing the same task ten times, you'll figure out what steps are essential and which can be cut back or eliminated, and what sequence of steps will produce the desired outcome most quickly and reliably.

But developing or acquiring new tools isn't just a matter of re-fining a known process. Experience might also guide you to seek new tools from an outside source, and in the process learn a new process, which will then in turn be refined with practice. Perhaps as you work in the lower ranks of an engineering firm, you con-clude that your undergraduate engineering degree hasn't prepared you to take on the work that most interests you. So you decide to return to school and pursue a master's in engineering, or perhaps an MBA, if the work that most interests you is management or product development.

Young's experience guided him to further deepen his pattern-recognition skills. When I asked him why the top-heavy IQs had so much trouble formulating a profitable business strategy, Young said the answer was "really straightforward. It's all pattern recog-nition, and they had no experience. They had no patterns to com-pare" their proposed strategy with known business results. His own capacity for making sound strategic decisions, he said, was largely a function of pattern recognition—which by definition requires experience. "It is all pattern recognition," he says, "and I've been around for several rounds."

As experience leads us to acquire new tools, we add depth and clarity to our stance. If our engineer enters business school and acquires the tools of an MBA, she modifies her view of her place in the world—her stance. No longer simply an engineer capable of tackling the technical aspects of a particular class of problems, she is an engineer with the business skills to view a wider range of problems with a broader perspective and address them with more diverse set of tools.

For Young, pattern recognition became the tool that was cen-tral to his stance—he was a sales guy whose experience enabled him to solve problems by recognizing their characteristic patterns. Thanks to his experiences, he grew more and more confident that he could see what was likely to transpire and to make bold decisions on the basis of the patterns he recognized—including the decision to give away Red Hat software over the Internet.

The dynamics of your personal knowledge system are graphically rendered in figure 5-1. Stance guides the acquisition of tools, and stance and tools shape experiences, which in turn inform tools, which in turn inform stance.

The circular relationship between stance and tools was famously noted by communications theorist and philosopher Marshall McLuhan, who in turn was paraphrasing an observation made by Sir Winston Churchill. McLuhan argued that, "We shape our tools and afterwards our tools shape us."[3] I agree entirely, but I wouldn't stop there. Our tools inform our experiences, which lead

FIGURE 5-1

Your personal knowledge system

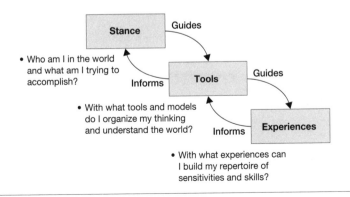

us to new tools, which expand or deepen or otherwise alter our stance. To follow McLuhan's thought all the way out to the end, then, we shape our tools and, through experience, practice, refine, and incorporate them into our stance. In due course, they shape us.

The late Sumantra Ghoshal, a London Business School professor, made a similar point in his critique of MBA education. He argued that the economic and game-theory tools that are staples of the business-school curriculum teach students to play zero-sum games—in other words, to see only trade-offs in the universe of possibilities. Their experience using those tools, Ghoshal argued, eventually shapes them into executives who know only how to play zero-sum games. Exposure to different tools and experiences, he maintained, would have shaped their stances much differently, producing executives who were not only capable of playing and winning positive-sum games, but able to recognize them in the first place.[4]

Beneficial and Detrimental Spirals

As Ghoshal's argument suggests, personal knowledge systems are highly path-dependent.[5] When a person starts in a given direction, that direction is likely to be reinforced and amplified, not diminished or altered. This can happen for good or bad; that is, the spiral can be beneficial or detrimental. Operating at their best, the three elements of the personal knowledge system will reinforce each other to produce an ever-increasing capacity for integrative thinking. By the same token, though, stance, tools, and experience can conspire to trap perfectly intelligent and capable people in a world where problems seem too hard to solve and mere survival is the only goal.

A narrow and defensive stance will lead to acquisition of extremely limited tools and extremely limiting experiences. Those experiences then feed back into the acquisition of even more limited tools and the formation of an even narrower stance. Imagine a young man of color born into a fractured, chaotic inner-city household. His early experience and upbringing teach him to see himself as an oppressed person in a world that offers him few opportunities to improve his circumstances. With little to hope for or aspire to, this young man's motivation is just to survive, and the tools he acquires are only those he thinks will enable him to survive. Using those tools exposes him to experiences that validate his initial view of himself as a person trapped in a world that offers no opportunities for escape or improvement. Under the circumstances, it's almost impossible for him to imagine acquiring better tools that might give him a more expansive view of life's possibilities.

Michael Lee-Chin's story shows how a different stance can set a person on a far different path. Although Lee-Chin grew up a mixed-race child from the mean streets of Port Antonio, he saw the world as full of opportunities and himself as an achiever motivated to succeed. His outlook motivated him to apply to colleges in North America, confident that he could obtain the financial aid he would need to attend. At college, he acquired tools that further expanded his sense of life's possibilities. He gained experience in investment management and continuously honed his sensitivities and skills. This experience reinforced his view of the world as a place in which his efforts would be rewarded, further strengthening his stance as someone capable of great success.

The spirals proceed powerfully in opposite directions. Lee-Chin's positive spiral made it obvious which tools he needed to acquire and which experiences would deepen his sensitivities and skills. His experiences, in turn, reinforced his desire to invest in acquiring further skills, enhancing his view of himself and his place in the world, and sharpening his motivation to shape his world for the better. The negative spiral of the hypothetical young man from the inner city, by contrast, generates defeatism. Beginning with image of the world as a miserable place, his stance, tools, and experience conspire to confirm his original view of the world as a place where the best you can do is second best.

Neither spiral is foreordained. Your personal knowledge system—your stance, tools, and experiences—is under your control. You have wide latitude as to how to develop your personal knowledge system. You might not be able to change your height, IQ, or DNA, but as long as you can change your stance, you can change the tools and experiences you use to develop your thinking capacity—especially your integrative thinking capacity.

The next three chapters address stance, tools, and experiences, respectively. Each component of the personal knowledge system is illustrated by stories of integrative thinkers. From there, I draw out the implications for developing your integrative thinking capacity and show how my colleagues and I are building these capacities in students and executives. The hope is that these three chapters will reinforce a positive spiral in your own personal knowledge system, propelling continuous improvement in your own integrative thinking capacity.

CHAPTER 6

The Construction Project

Imagining Reality

It is impossible to begin to learn that which one thinks one already knows.

—Epictetus (c. 55–c. 135)

"UNACCEPTABLE!" In a ninety-minute conversation, that was the only word that Victoria Hale, the founder of the Institute for OneWorld Heath (IOWH), spat out in disgust. She uttered thousands of words in the course of my interview with her, words by turns emotional, reflective, analytical, funny, charming. But when the conversation turned to the pharmaceutical industry's failure to address the needs of the poor, and the medical profession's shrugging acceptance of that state of affairs, Hale let fly with a sentence that carried an explosive charge of contempt for laziness, complacency, and the status quo: "It was *unacceptable* to me as a pharmaceutical scientist."[1]

Hale isn't just any pharmaceutical scientist. Trained in the world-renowned pharmaceutical chemistry PhD program at the University of California at San Francisco, she has worked as a senior reviewer of new-drug applications at the U.S. Food and Drug Administration and as a scientist at Genentech, the world's leading biotech company. She was on a path to a senior leadership position, either in government or at a major pharmaceutical company, but in 2000, at the age of forty, she stepped off that path to found IOWH, the world's first not-for-profit pharmaceutical company. IOWH's mission: to change the way in which drugs are developed—or more to the point, *not* developed—for diseases afflicting the world's poor.

Over the course of her career in pharmaceuticals, Hale had learned that the industry had two ways of getting drugs to the people who need them. The first was the traditional for-profit pharmaceutical model: A drug company spends billions of dollars to develop a pharmaceutical treatment for a particular disease or condition, a process that takes years of lab work and clinical trials. If, at the end of this process, a drug gains regulatory approval, the pharmaceutical company sells it for a price that covers its costs and earns an acceptable profit for its shareholders. The second approach, known as the public health model, involves using subsidies, either from governments or pharmaceutical companies themselves, to make expensive drugs affordable for poor patients.

Both models have their strengths. The for-profit model mobilizes hundreds of billions of dollars in capital to find new drugs for endemic diseases. The public health model leverages government and pharmaceutical company resources to help millions of people buy drugs they can't otherwise afford. But neither model addresses the massive needs of people in the poorest countries. For-profit pharmaceutical companies develop new drugs for people who can afford them. They have no incentive to address diseases that primarily affect poor people, because the drugs to treat these people won't generate enough revenue for their developers to recoup their research and distribution costs.

Don't take that as an indictment of the drug companies. They're not greedy or heartless, but as public, for-profit corporations, they're constrained by their obligations to their shareholders and employees. There's not much future in targeting customers who can't pay.

The public health model brings the cost of existing drugs within the reach of millions of poor people. But the public health market can only expand the market for existing drugs; it can't bring new drugs into existence. Public health organizations aren't in the drug-development business themselves, and they can't offer the for-profit companies sufficient economic incentives to focus on diseases that primarily affect poor people.

Between the two models, then, lies a vast gap in which major killing diseases flourish, with no attempt to find a pharmaceutical solution. That's unacceptable to Hale. She told me that as she studied the problem of developing drugs for poor populations, she asked herself, "Why couldn't there be a not-for-profit pharmaceutical company? If we could put together the technology and the people and the resources to get through the development stage and we had a product in the end that would be affordable . . . Let's try it. Let's put it together." And thus the IOWH was formed.

The next step was to zero in on a disease afflicting poor people that would be susceptible to pharmaceutical intervention. One candidate was visceral leishmaniasis, a parasitic disease concentrated in poorest Bangladesh, India, Nepal, Brazil, and Sudan that kills about five hundred thousand people a year, making it the second biggest parasitic disease killer in the world after malaria. Those infected with *kala-azar* (literally, black fever), as it's known in the local Indian parlance, die a slow, agonizing death as the parasite destroys their internal organs. The disease is curable by a full course of an antibiotic known as amphotericin B, but its cost—more than the lifetime earnings of most black fever sufferers—places that cure beyond the reach of all but a lucky few.

Hale and her IOWH colleagues launched a search for an affordable treatment for black fever. Before long, they found a drug that looked as if it might be effective. Paromomycin was an antibiotic that was brought to market in 1961 and discontinued about fifteen years later when it was no longer profitable. Hale and IOWH hit the foundation circuit to raise enough money to carry out a large-scale clinical test of paromomycin's effectiveness against black fever, in cooperation with the Indian government.

IOWH's phase-three clinical trial concluded in November 2004, with researchers reporting that 95 percent of patients given paromomycin were cured. In August 2006, the Drug-Controller General of India approved paromomycin to treat black fever in India. Because the cost is a mere $10 per patient for a full course of treatment, the government of India was able to cover the entire cost for its citizens. IOWH is lobbying the other countries with large numbers of black fever sufferers to follow suit.

With the support of the Indian government, IOWH is now working with partner Gland Pharma Limited of India to produce and distribute paromomycin across India. For her part in achieving this breakthrough, Hale was named Outstanding Social Entrepreneur by the Schwab Foundation in 2004 and Executive of the Year by *Esquire* magazine in 2005. She was awarded *The Economist* Innovation Award for Social and Economic Innovation in

2005 and the Skoll Award for Social Entrepreneurship in 2005. In 2006, she won a MacArthur Fellowship, known colloquially as a genius grant. It's given to individuals who demonstrate, in the MacArthur Foundation's words, "exceptional creativity [and] promise for important future advances based on a track record of significant accomplishment." [2]

If there was an award for excellence in integrative thinking, she'd win that, too. After all, she forged a creative resolution of two entrenched business models—one that was brilliantly successful at developing drugs but was structurally unsuited to serving low-income markets, and another that served low-income markets well but was structurally unsuited to developing new drugs. Rather than simply accepting the limitations of either model, Hale took personal responsibility for devising something better. She used her opposable mind to bring something new to the world: a not-for-profit pharmaceutical company. The question I want to explore in this chapter is: What stances do Victoria Hale and other integrative thinkers take that drive them toward creative resolutions?

The Integrative Thinker's Stance

Integrative thinkers are a varied lot, as we've seen. But their stances have in common six key features. Three concern the world around them; three concern their role in it. First, they believe that whatever models exist at the present moment do not represent reality; they are simply the best or only constructions yet made. As Hale said of the state of pharmaceutical development before IOWH entered the picture: "This is reality? It's the way things are? No! No! There's a much messier situation behind that and around that and enmeshed in that."

Second, they believe that conflicting models, styles, and approaches to problems are to be leveraged, not feared. "We have some individuals who are very pharmaceutical and very technical and not oriented to fieldwork," Hale told me, "and then we have some individuals who are very field-oriented and relationship-oriented and culturally sensitive and not technically oriented or trained. But we need all of that to come together to make this world."

Third, they believe that better models exist that are not yet seen. Hale described how she responded to fellow scientists who dismissed her idea for IOWH before she had even attempted it: "I would say, 'How can you, as a scientist, say that?' Sure, this is a huge undertaking, but if no one has ever tried it, how can you conclude that it won't work? We have to do the experiment."

Fourth, they believe that not only does a better model exist, but that they are capable of bringing that better model from abstract hypothesis to concrete reality. "I viewed [the problem of drug development for poor populations] first as a scientist, and said to myself and to others, 'We should try it,'" she said. "My verbs are important here: We should. We *should* try it. And then, I actually *can* try it. And then, I *will* try it. And then I *am* trying it."

Fifth, they are comfortable wading into complexity to ferret out a new and better model, confident they will emerge on the other side with the resolution they seek. "I can see a big picture, and I can imagine, and fear doesn't come with that," Hale said. "I can go deep, and I can go wide. While I'm disrupting my world and looking for mess, I'm actually looking for peace and calm. I'm not afraid of the mess."

And sixth, they give themselves the time to create a better model. "I will know what I need to do when the time is right," Hale said. "I just know. Whenever I have wanted to know, I gave it the time and the space and the energy—it takes substantial work. I just stay with it, sit with it, spin it around. You can't rush it. You know, it happens when it happens."

This is an inherently optimistic stance. Integrative thinkers understand that the world imposes constraints on them, but they share the belief that with hard thinking and patience, they can find a better outcome than the unsatisfying ones they're presented with.

We have already seen Isadore Sharp of Four Seasons look at the existing business models for the hotel business and come up with something better: "the best of small motels combined with the best of large hotels." We have seen Tim Brown determine that IDEO designs had to satisfy users' functional and emotional requirements simultaneously, instead of trading off one for the other.

K. V. Kamath took the helm of a small Indian government-backed development bank in 1996 and turned it into ICICI Bank. ICICI swiftly grew to dominate retail banking in India and is now globalizing rapidly and taking on the world's long-established banks and winning. Like Sharp and Brown, Kamath rejected conventional wisdom, which held that he faced an irresolvable trade-off, in this case between quality and efficiency. He has structured and managed ICICI Bank to achieve both aims.

Most integrative thinkers quite explicitly refuse to accept trade-offs that the rest of the world tells them are unavoidable. Meg Whitman, CEO of eBay, is typical. She describes the secret of eBay as "this idea of 'and.' It's not just community for community's sake, and it's not just commerce for commerce's sake. It's the two of these things combined, which is quite powerful."[3] Nandan Nilekani, the builder and CEO of what is perhaps India's most successful global IT powerhouse, Infosys Technologies Limited, says that when he's confronted with two fundamentally opposed sets of requirements, his first inclination is to ask, "Are there solutions that satisfy both?"[4] And when asked whether he thought strategy or execution was more important, Jack Welch, the former chairman and CEO of General Electric, responded, "I don't think it's an either-or."[5]

Integrative thinkers also share an uncanny composure in the face of complexity. They wait patiently for the multifarious strands of a problem to become apparent and shape themselves into some kind of pattern. Ramalinga Raju uses a rich metaphor to describe the process. Raju founded Satyam Computer Services in 1988. Since then it has grown to more than $1 billion in sales and thirty-five thousand employees around the world. "If you are swimming on the surface," he said, "then you are very unlikely to find pearls, because they are deep underneath and you have to dive down; you have to go into a fair amount of depth on any particular issue that you take up." And what, I asked him, is your process for depth-diving when you're faced with a complex problem involving clashing models? "I meditate," he said.[6]

Such meditations produce solutions that, in the words of Bruce Mau of Bruce Mau Design, "revolve around the plural."[7] At the core of every integrative thinker's stance is a predisposition to look at models together, not separately, in search for useful answers. Such thinking is the very embodiment of Thomas C. Chamberlin's idea of multiple working hypotheses.

Cultivating Stance

As we proceed to the work of cultivating a stance, remember that stance is not, as it were, freestanding. It exists only in the context of tools and experiences, which require time to accumulate. So neither I nor anyone else can teach you the stance of an integrative thinker. Such a stance is a cumulative continuous process that begins with the individual temperament (think here of Michael Lee-Chin's bedrock belief that the world was susceptible to his efforts to change it). Tools and experiences reinforce the stance entailed by temperament, and they add depth and nuance.

The question, then, is what initial features of stance can serve as the foundation of a personal knowledge system that we then build into the robust stance of an integrative thinker like Victoria Hale?

The foundations are the six elements of stance that I introduced earlier in this chapter. We're about to discuss them at some length, so let's review them now:

STANCE ABOUT THE WORLD

1. Existing models do not represent reality; they are our constructions.

2. Opposing models are to be leveraged, not feared.

3. Existing models are not perfect; better models exist that are not yet seen.

4. I am capable of finding a better model.

5. I can wade into and get through the necessary complexity.

6. I give myself the time to create a better model.

As you look over the entries on this list, remember that each is only a start. They have to be reinforced with tools and experiences to become robust. As your integrative thinking stance takes root and develops flexibility and strength, you'll also discover that each element in the stance about the self has a counterpart in the stance about the world. As you come to understand that existing models do not represent reality, you'll also begin to believe you are capable of finding a better model. As you learn to see that opposing models exist to be leveraged, you'll grow more comfortable wading into the resulting complexity, confident that you'll come out the other side with deeper understanding. And as your conviction grows that better models exist that are not yet seen, you'll find yourself more willing to take the time you need to fashion a creative resolution.

So if stance itself cannot be taught, its elements can. Let's see how, beginning with the first one.

1. Existing Models Do Not Represent Reality

As discussed in chapter 3, we come to the world with a "factory setting" that causes us to confuse our perceptions, which are subjective constructions, with objective reality. The confusion is reinforced every time we hear someone say, "The reality is . . ." It's further reinforced by our education, which drills us to recall facts on demand, even when those facts are actually interpretations, whether of a Shakespeare play or the Battle of Waterloo or Karl Marx's theory of surplus capital. This isn't the result of a grand conspiracy to plant in our minds a permanent confusion between constructions and reality. It's just the nature of factory settings to seek to perpetuate themselves, and this particular setting has found a way to flourish in our educational system.

The first step toward a consciously cultivated stance is to learn to distinguish between subjective constructions and objective reality. The movie *Crash*, winner of the Academy Award for Best Picture of 2005 (as well as two other Oscars), vividly shows how that distinction can be, quite literally, a matter of life and death.

The plot of *Crash* weaves together several vignettes of super-charged racial tension in Los Angeles. One crucial strand of the plot is the escalating confrontation between Daniel, a Hispanic locksmith, and Farhad, an Iranian shopkeeper. Farhad is a relatively recent immigrant who speaks heavily accented and rudimentary English and runs a modest shop in a poor neighborhood of Los Angeles. Thieves have broken into the shop or held him up several times, and he eventually decides to buy a gun for protection, against the entreaties of his highly assimilated daughter, Dorri, who is pursuing a medical degree. Farhad's English isn't good enough to manage the transaction with the gun shop owner, and so despite her misgivings, Dorri helps her father buy the gun.

When we see Farhad again, he's on the phone to his insurance company, complaining that his shop isn't secure because the back door lock is broken. The insurance company sends Daniel, an independent contractor who works as a twenty-four-hour on-call locksmith. Daniel, a twenty-something Latino, is, well, a little scary-looking, especially to a cultural outsider like Farhad. Daniel's head is shaved bald, he wears an earring and has several prominent tattoos, and he dresses like a member of one of the local gangs that plague Farhad's impoverished neighborhood.

But in a few economical scenes, we glimpse another side of Daniel: a gentle family man who treasures his wife and young daughter. The family lives in a modest but immaculate house—he takes his shoes off before he enters. We see the pride his five-year-old daughter takes in her school uniform, and we gather that Daniel and his wife have made deep sacrifices to send their girl to a private school.

The first lesson dramatists learn is that every scene contains some form of conflict. The crucial scene between Daniel and Farhad is *all* conflict, a clash between two subjective constructions of reality so completely at odds with each other, as well as with objective reality, that a tragic denouement is all but inevitable.

The scene opens in Farhad's shop. Daniel is in back, working on the faulty lock. He turns away from his labors and approaches Farhad, who is sitting at the cash register listening to Iranian music, his mind seemingly far away.

"Excuse me," Daniel says. "Excuse me, sir." Farhad is plainly irritated to be distracted from his reverie. "You finished?" he asks brusquely.

"I replaced the lock," Daniel says, "but you got a real problem with that door."

"You fixed the lock?" Farhad inquires impatiently.

"Nah, I replaced the lock," Daniel says. "But you gotta fix that door."

"Just fix the lock," Farhad snaps.

"Sir, listen to me," Daniel says, his patience fraying at the edges. "What you need is a new door."

"I need new door?"

"Yeah."

"Okay. How much?"

"I don't," Daniel begins, then shakes his head. "Sir, you're gonna have to call somebody that sells doors."

"You try to cheat me, right?" Farhad asks aggressively. "You have a friend that fix door?"

"Nah, I don't have a friend that fixes doors, bro," Daniel says. He's offended, and angry.

"Then go and fix the #$&★@ lock, you cheater!"

"Y-y-y-you know what?" Daniel says. He's nearing his breaking point. "Why don't you just pay for the lock and I won't charge you for the time?" He hands Farhad a copy of the work order.

"You don't fix the lock," Farhad says, slamming the paperwork down on the counter, "I pay? What? You think I am stupid? You fix the #$&★@ lock, you cheater."

"Now, I'd appreciate it if you stop calling me names," Daniel says, controlling himself with effort.

"Then fix the #$&★@ lock!" Farhad demands.

"I replaced the lock! You gotta fix the #$&★@ door!"

"You cheat! You #$&★@ cheater!"

"Fine," Daniels says, crumpling the work order. "Don't pay."

"What?" Farhad says, staring in disbelief as Daniel throws the balled-up paper in the trash.

"Have a good night," Daniel says sarcastically and turns to walk toward the door.

"What?" Farhad says, furious. "No, wait. Wait. You come back here. You fix the lock. Come here you, fix my lock."

But Daniel is already out the door.

The next morning, Farhad goes to open his store, only to find that it's been broken into and trashed. To add racist insult to Farhad's injury, the vandals have spray-painted anti-Arab graffiti all over the walls, with vengeful references to the 9/11 attacks. This doubles Farhad's fury—he's Persian and regards being called Arab as a grave insult. He is devastated.

Farhad's outrage is complete when the insurance adjuster informs him that the insurer won't cover the damage. Farhad was negligent, the adjuster explains, in not taking Daniel's advice to have the door fixed.

As he broods on this injustice, Farhad becomes convinced that Daniel was responsible for the break-in. Using the address he finds on the crumpled work order that Daniel threw in Farhad's trash can, he goes to Daniel's house with the gun his daughter helped him buy. In due course, Daniel pulls his locksmith's van into his driveway. As he steps out of the van, Farhad confronts him, gun in hand. He demands his money back. Daniel doesn't understand what he is talking about. He tries to placate Farhad, but his efforts only inflame Farhad further.

From the front window of the house, Daniel's young daughter watches the confrontation unfold. She rushes out to protect her father, only to step directly into the line of fire just as Farhad shoots at Daniel. Daniel screams in agony, and his wife, who has just raced outside from the kitchen, falls to her knees at the front steps, sobbing.

The scene, in which an innocent little girl becomes the victim of a wholly preventable misunderstanding, is almost unbearably tragic. But the confrontation between Daniel and Farhad takes a surprising twist, thanks to Dorri, Farhad's daughter. In a startling scene later in the film, we learn that while helping her father buy the gun and ammunition, she surreptitiously bought blanks. Those were blanks that Farhad fired at the man he wrongly thought had cheated him and violated his property. The lives of Daniel and his daughter are spared, and Farhad is spared a first-degree murder charge.

This compelling scene speaks directly to the importance of a stance that consciously distinguishes between reality and its many subjective models. Both Daniel and Farhad develop models of each other that they see as coterminous with reality. Their models are so real to them that they are willing to take extreme action on them. Farhad's actions may be more extreme than Daniel's, but both men go too far.

In Farhad's mind, Daniel is first a cheater, then a full-fledged criminal who either broke in himself or gave the address to his criminal friends to do the dirty work. What data was salient to him? Daniel's ethnicity, his menacing appearance, and his inability to fix the door. Farhad made causal links among that data to construct a model of Daniel as a cheater who invented a problem with the door to get work for one of his friends. That model shapes his understanding of his confrontation with the cheater. Daniel's anger, refusal to finish the job, and the subsequent vandalizing of the store are all salient data points that reinforce and amplify his initial construction of Daniel's character: this dangerous-looking locksmith is a cheater—a *criminal* cheater.

As Farhad is constructing his model of Daniel, Daniel is constructing a model of Farhad. Salient to Daniel is the strange music

Farhad is listening to, his heavy accent, his awkwardly phrased accusation ("You try to cheat me, right?"). From these points of salience, he builds a model of an ignorant, belligerent, insulting man. He keeps his cool after Farhad accuses him, but the ironic, unfriendly spin he puts on the word "bro" ratchets up the hostilities. Daniel's language reinforces Farhad's view of him as some kind of gangster, and he steps up the volume and venom of his verbal attacks. Daniel, in his turn, reads Farhad's mounting anger as further confirmation of his original view of him as an ignorant hothead. He gives up on getting paid and walks out—confirming Farhad's view that Daniel can't be trusted.

Both Daniel and Farhad confuse their constructions of each other with reality itself, and those constructions determine each man's course of action. Certain that he was dealing with an ignorant, insulting, and belligerent man, Daniel felt justified in quickly giving up his effort to explain the problem with the door and leaving without helping the customer secure his premises.

Although Farhad had acted provocatively, Daniel's reaction wasn't foreordained. Before quickly cutting off any effort at communication and mutual understanding, he could have asked himself if there was an alternative explanation for Farhad's behavior. He could have decided that he needed to hang in there longer in order to figure out whether his initial construction of Farhad was right or wrong; he might have tried a different tack. He might have asked Farhad to come over to the door and shown him why the door, and not the lock, was at the root of the problem. Instead, he flung Farhad's curses back at him and stormed out in a huff, inadvertently giving Farhad another data point for his erroneous, or at least seriously incomplete, construction of Daniel. To

Farhad, Daniel was obviously angry enough to return with his lowlife friends and trash his store.

But if Daniel's error lay in what he didn't do, Farhad's error lay in what he did, which was far more extreme than Daniel's angry exit. Because Farhad's constructed model of Daniel led him to believe Daniel was the author of the break-in, Farhad believed he was justified in shooting that cheating criminal. Just like Daniel, Farhad could have asked himself it was possible to put a different construction on Daniel's conduct. Even the pause to think might have dissuaded him from racing off for revenge, gun in hand.

The point here, as I tell my students, is that reality isn't all it's cracked up to be. Very little in life should be viewed as incontrovertibly real. We're usually connected to reality by our model of it. Once, for example, Sir Isaac Newton's model of the forces governing the universe was commonly taken as reality itself. It was an almost palpable wrench for educated people when Albert Einstein proposed a superior model of physical forces. The forces hadn't changed, but the systematic description of them had, and it left many people feeling as if the forces themselves had come unstuck.

If there's an overriding lesson to take away from the story of Daniel and Farhad, it's that (1) anything we think is real is actually a model of reality; and (2) that model is probably imperfect in some important respects.

2. *Opposing Models Are to Be Leveraged, Not Feared*

There's much to be gained from the recognition that no model has a lock on reality, but that all models reflect reality from a particular angle. It becomes possible to assemble a fuller, though probably not complete, model of reality by incorporating a variety of other models. Salient data that was once overlooked, causal patterns that formerly went unnoticed, architectural possibilities that once went unexplored, all begin to emerge.

Opposing models, in fact, are the richest source of new insight into a problem. We learn nothing from someone who sees the problem exactly as we do. The agreement and reinforcement are gratifying, but that sense of gratification can be deceiving if we both have overlooked something crucial. Farhad and Daniel could have learned a lot from each other, and they hurt themselves by giving up on the effort. The most creative, productive stance is one that sees opposing models as learning opportunities to be appreciated, welcomed, and understood.

Models, integrative thinkers realize, are bound to clash, just as they do in the story of Sally and Bill, recounted in chapter 3. Some degree of conflict occurs every time two or more people look at a particular slice of reality and try to model it. So there's no reason to be alarmed when each story has as many competing realities as it has participants and witnesses; there's no need to go to battle stations as Farhad and Daniel or Sally and Bill do. If anything but your model is wrong, every other model is a problem to be eliminated or ignored. If instead your model is one of many, all of them imperfect, then the existence of a clashing version is to be expected, not feared.

3. Better Models Exist That Are Not Yet Seen

The next step in teaching integrative thinking is to cultivate the belief that better models exist that are not yet seen.

At the broadest level, there are two conceptual approaches for considering and evaluating theories of how the world works. I call them the "contented model defense" and "optimistic model seeking." Contented model defense is by far the most prevalent model—it is the factory setting for most people, who are generally unconscious of its operation. When we engage in contented model defense, we adopt a theory and then seek to support and defend it. As we accumulate data in support of the theory we've adopted, we become more certain that our theory represents the truth and more content that we have achieved our ultimate goal, certainty.[8]

Recall now the scene between Farhad and Daniel. Both engage in contented model defense. Farhad quickly built a model of Daniel—the cheater model—then looked for evidence to confirm the veracity of his model: Daniel called him "bro"; Daniel swore at him; Daniel refused to come back and fix the door; Daniel stormed out in anger. All of these things confirmed in Farhad's mind that Daniel was a cheater at best and a criminal at worst.

Simultaneously, Daniel was forming a model of Farhad as ignorant and insulting: Farhad called him a cheater; Farhad swore at him; Farhad yelled at him. All of these things confirmed Daniel's derogatory model of Farhad.

The problem with single-mindedly seeking to justify and confirm the veracity of the existing model is that the contented model defender won't treat disconfirming data as valid, much less salient. When we go into defensive mode, we short-circuit any attempt to seek a more accurate model. Had he wanted to see it, Farhad could have found plenty of data to disconfirm his model of Daniel. If Daniel was a cheater, why was he so quick to offer not to charge for his labor?

Daniel, for his part, had less data to disconfirm his model of Farhad, but he had some. After all, Farhad persisted in asking

Daniel to come back and fix the lock. Viewed charitably, he was crying out, albeit ineffectively, for someone to clear up his confusion about the door and the lock. Had Daniel not gotten angry and walked out, the misunderstanding could have been resolved without violence.

In many respects, Chamberlin offers the most effective counterargument to the contented model defense, with his admonitions against the "ruling theory" approach to scientific work. Contented model defenders want to have a ruling theory because when it's confirmed, they can return to a resting state, all their certainties in place. The reigning Western model of education, with its emphasis on finding a single right answer, supports this tendency.

Within the contented model defense stance, an alternative or clashing model is a problem to be eliminated. Alternative models pose a threat to the veracity of the existing model and must be disbelieved, distorted, and disproved. Farhad's model didn't allow for the possibility that Daniel genuinely wanted to help him fix his problem. Daniel's offer not to charge for his labor challenged the accuracy of Farhad's model of Daniel as a cheater, so Farhad felt compelled to reject the possibility that Daniel meant well. Seeing Daniel's loving household would have posed another challenge to Farhad's model, so he didn't seek out that disconfirming data. The existing model had to be protected and justified.

There is a more productive alternative to defending one existing model against all challenges: the stance of the optimistic model seeker. The optimistic model seeker doesn't believe there is a right answer, just the best answer available now. American philosopher Charles Sanders Peirce (1839–1914) called this the fallibilist stance, because it presumes that all models are fallible.[9] That doesn't mean that current models should be rejected. Until the best present model is eclipsed by a better model, the best present model should govern. But fallibilism assumes that the best current model will be eclipsed in due course, as will its successor models.

For optimistic model seekers, their resting state is not certainty. They are forever testing what they think they know against the best available data. Their goal is the refutation of their current belief, because refutation represents not failure but an advance. Just as Peirce suggested, each new model, while an improvement, is still imperfect and replaceable in due course with a still-better model. In essence, the stance can be characterized as optimistic because it implies optimism that future models will be superior to the current model.

Optimistic model seeking reinforces and empowers the integrative thinking stance. Integrative thinkers look for and enjoy opposing models because they see the presence of an opposing model as evidence that a better model can and will emerge. Unlike contented model defenders, who are discomfited by multiple models, optimistic model seekers are discomfited by the presence of a single model. They see the value in the complexity of multiple models, and their preference is always to wait for a better model to emerge rather than to justify the existing model.

Many of the integrative thinkers I interviewed were explicit and conscious in their optimistic model seeking. Bob Young of Red Hat loves being challenged and enlightened by a model that stands in opposition to the conventional wisdom. "When any asset is dismissed by others," Young says, "it is a sign that it should probably be purchased."[10] Michael Lee-Chin of AIC Limited takes a similar view of out-of-favor securities.[11] K. V. Kamath of ICICI Bank, while a supreme technologist, is suspicious of standard rules of thumb for technology. His goal at ICICI Bank was to match the IT capabilities of the bank's international competitors but at a tenth of their cost, and that meant telling his IT department to toss out the standard models for how to build and manage a bank IT infrastructure.[12]

Perhaps the most flamboyant of the optimistic model seekers was Rob McEwen, the former CEO of Goldcorp.[13] McEwen is famous within the staid gold mining industry, and now far beyond it, for applying the open-source ethos of the Linux movement to the mining industry. He put all of Goldcorp's geological information about its Red Lake mine on the Internet and offered prizes for the best ideas on where Goldcorp should drill for gold. McEwen's rivals thought he was nuts, but that didn't stop him. The ideas from McEwen's Internet challenge transformed Goldcorp's Red Lake mine from an underperforming asset to the most productive gold mine in the industry.

McEwen's description of the stance underlying his decision is telling. "I was looking," he says, "for the fundamental, underlying, unquestioned assumption that everybody in the industry grows up with. And if you find that assumption, and then question it, you can start seeing opportunities. If you can define the problem differently than everybody else in the industry, you can generate alternatives that others aren't thinking about."

Implicit in McEwen's stance is his fundamental optimism that there is a better model out there. To cultivate a similar stance, we must first become aware of our own tendency to resort to contented model defense. Next, we need to come to see optimistic model seeking as a legitimate approach.

The first step, then, is to examine our own personal beliefs and determine how and why we maintain them. Typically, we find that we maintain our beliefs by engaging in contented model defense. For example, we often resort to authority to justify our beliefs. "I know it is true because that is the way God meant it to be" is an example of that defensive strategy. Invoking divine authority neatly blocks any search for inconsistent or disconfirming data—such a search would be tantamount to blasphemy.

Logical circularity is another favorite strategy of contented model defenders. "I know that I treated him fairly in that transaction," we tell ourselves, "because I am a fair person." This formulation neatly places the burden of error on the person who feels unfairly treated.

Most of us entertain such beliefs without examining them closely. In the integrative thinking course I teach at the Rotman School, students learn to examine the logic behind their own beliefs. They're usually surprised to discover that they can and do hold models to be true on the basis of little or no testing or evidence.

4. I Am Capable of Finding a Better Model

The three stance statements concerning the self are harder to teach than the three elements of stance about the world. While one may believe that being an optimistic model seeker is superior and want desperately to be one, the desire does not automatically produce the desired outcome. In truth, experience is the best teacher of these components of stance, because only through experience do we gain confidence that the statements are indeed true. And only through experience do we gain skill and confidence that we can find the better model, handle complexity, and be patient with ourselves. But we can help by teaching our students to reflect on how they think consciously and systematically. Through reflection they learn to explore the thinking that goes into their decisions. They learn to analyze the models underlying their decision to determine what was salient and what causal relationships were inferred. And by analyzing their decisions, students learn whether they were able to focus on the whole as they designed a solution, or whether, like most of us, they got lost along the way, emphasizing one detail at the expense of the whole.

To learn from our decisions and their consequences, we must be explicit in advance about the thought process preceding the decision. For better and for worse, the mind has an almost infinite capacity for rationalizing after the fact. If things don't go the way we hoped they would, we are capable of totally forgetting the thoughts that led to our decision. Instead, we tell ourselves that the unanticipated outcome is, in fact, what we expected all along.

Corporate managers do this every day. They make investments in the expectation of a productive outcome. When the outcome is disappointing, they convince themselves that it couldn't have turned out otherwise—in fact, it was exactly what they were expecting all along. The only way to defeat that rationalizing mechanism is to record the thinking that leads to a decision and the outcome we expect from that decision. At that point, it's a fairly simple matter to compare the actual outcome against our expectations. The disparity—and there's almost sure to be a disparity—offers us a valuable glimpse into our own thought process and our characteristic errors—errors which are, I suggest, the product of our stance.

We ask students (some of whom are corporate executives) to practice optimistic model seeking by exploring a dilemma that features opposing models. I recently taught an integrative thinking workshop for the global human resources team of a large company. Their dilemma was whether to centralize their corporation's training and development globally or to distribute it, whether by region or by business unit.

I began by asking the group to "reverse engineer" the logic of both competing models. By reverse engineering, I meant I wanted them to trace the logical audit trail from salient data to causal connections to architecture of the model to its conclusions. But I wanted them to trace backward, from conclusion back to salient data.

When a group reverse engineers the assumptions underlying a given model it is important that the group's members focus on what would have to be true for the model to be valid, rather than what *they* think is true. By taking the time to consider what would have to be true for the model to be valid, they gain practice in not rushing to confirm or disconfirm the veracity of one model or the other.

In the human resources case, reverse engineering revealed that several things had to be true for the centralized model to be valid. The needs of the various regions had to be fairly similar. The central training unit had to have a good understanding of the needs of each region, despite the central unit's physical and cultural distance from the regions. The central unit would also have to gain buy-in from the key actors in the region.

For the distributed model, other conditions had to hold true. The individual training centers would have to be able to maintain reasonable cost-effectiveness without global scale. They'd have to maintain sufficient consistency in training and development across the whole firm. They'd have to be in close enough contact with corporate human resources to focus on the correct firmwide needs and priorities.

The participants were then asked to marshal two sorts of data. One set would support each statement of what would have to be true. Another set would undermine each statement. Seeking out disconfirming or undermining data was crucial to the exercise, because we want to avoid slipping into contented model defense.

As I expected, the class found that neither model was perfect. Some data supported each pillar of what would have to be true; some data disconfirmed it. For example, it was pretty clear that it was unlikely that the central unit could gain the respect of the key actors in the region. They thought that the central unit was inflexible and didn't understand the local training needs. Similarly, it was pretty clear that the distributed model wouldn't attain the consistency required for the company as a whole to maintain uniform standards. When the disconfirming data was laid out so clearly, defenders of each model had to concede the deficiencies of their favorite.

At the end of this exercise, the group had a clearer understanding that neither of their initial models was perfect. At that point they were prepared to entertain the suggestion that a better model awaited their discovery. More important, the thorough reverse engineering of the logic underlying both models helped them see that both models were constructions of reality and not reality itself. When the group understood that point, it was easier for them to consider the possibility that they might discover or devise better models.

The workshop participants came to understand that the global model was inflexible and couldn't allow for regional customization. The regional model lacked consistency and cost-efficiency. But they began to believe it wasn't necessary to trade off the advantages of each model against its disadvantages.

Together, the class worked to design an integrative resolution to the training dilemma. After some struggle and trial and error, a better model emerged by which a centralized global function would create, to borrow a metaphor from IT, training content "platforms." The regions could then efficiently build custom "applications" on top of those platforms. The global platforms would ensure consistency and capture economies of scale. The local applications would ensure that the training was right for the regions and give the regions sense of ownership, which was crucial to the success of the effort.

In hindsight, the solution appears simple, if not downright simplistic. Yet the participants in the class had not arrived at the solution before we undertook our exercise in reverse engineering. And it's unlikely that they would have discovered the solution if the members of the human resources team had remained in contented model defense mode. They would have been looking only at data that supported whatever model they were rooting for and would have missed out on the advantages of the model they didn't favor, as well as the shortcomings of the model they did favor. By shifting to an optimistic model-seeking approach, the class was able to analyze the opposing models dispassionately and gain the insight needed to devise the new model. And the discovery of the new and better model gave the participants confidence not only that there was a better model out there, but that they were fully capable of finding it.

5. I Can Wade into and Get Through the Necessary Complexity

To build the confidence and skill in wading into complexity to get to the other side—as did Victoria Hale—we teach students in the integrative thinking course at Rotman a version of the reverse engineering that the HR team engaged in. The students build backward from outcomes, to the actions that produced the outcomes, to the thinking behind the actions. We call this sequence

Thinking → Actions → Outcomes,

or TAO.

To teach students how to follow this sequence, my colleagues and I ask them to play a standard business simulation game. The game consists of eight teams, or companies, each starting in the same position. They play four periods, which represent four years of operations for each company. Each team chooses the region (one of four) in which it will produce its theoretical product, how much it will produce, how much it will advertise, how much it will invest in research and development, and at what level it will set its prices. In short, each team must design a complicated sequence of actions in a complex environment and has limited time to do so.[14] They submit new choices at each round, and a computer simulation runs the algorithms to determine the outcome.

Unlike many business school exercises, this is a complex and ambiguous game with no predetermined right answer. And as quickly becomes clear, the results of each team's choices are dependent to some degree on the choices of the other teams.

Things never turn out as the students expected. After they finish the game, we ask each team to pick one outcome they found particularly disappointing. What action or actions, we ask, led most directly to this unhappy outcome? What thinking led to the action or actions?

Working backward through the action sequence enables students to see where they've missed salient data or overlooked a crucial causal sequence. One team was most disappointed by its third-period sales. In analyzing the action that produced the poor sales results, the team found that they had sought too large a profit margin. In consequence, they ended up pricing themselves out of the market.

Was it simple greed that led to the pricing error, or did the team miss salient market information? In thinking backward along the causal chain, they realized that they had misinterpreted the pricing signals that emerged from the preceding period. They thought that every team would be content to walk prices upward in a straight line, but in fact, some teams opted to slash prices in the third period in order to gain volume and market share. By not considering the competitive environment in all its complexity, with all its many points of salience, this team invited disappointment.

The participants in these classes learn three things quite quickly. First, they learn that they don't think about their thinking much. Second, they learn that thinking about their thinking—reflecting, in other words—is hard. The teams struggle mightily to put together the

Thinking → Actions → Outcomes

chain. Even

Actions → Outcomes

is hard for them. Typically, outcomes just occur and those responsible for the actions that produced them quickly forget what they did, focusing instead on the next series of actions.

If working backward from outcomes to actions is difficult, delving one level further back to the thinking that produced the action is harder still. Few students, whatever their age or level of attainment, have much experience reflecting on their own thinking.

Third, they learn that systematically reflecting on how they think is a powerful way to change how they think. It's very common to hear students exclaim, when they complete an exercise in reverse engineering, "What were we thinking?" Such moments of profound incredulity—and insight—come only from thinking about thinking.

One powerful lesson in thinking about thinking emerged when we were running two games simultaneously (we had an especially large crop of students). A key choice that each team must make in the first period is where to build its plant. Each team can have only one plant, which can be expanded but not moved. Here again, the students learned the importance of taking into consideration the potential choices of the other teams. Absent such consideration, the obvious choice is to build the plant in North America, the biggest market with the most favorable average shipping costs to the other three regions.

Remember we had two games running simultaneously. In one of the games, four teams sited their plants in North America, three in Europe, and one in Asia—a productive mix as it turns out. In the other game, all eight plants were sited in North America, which set off brutal head-to-head competition. The teams in the second game all earned substandard profits, because they were all competing viciously in the North American home market, with aggressive price cuts the weapon of choice. The teams playing the other game, where there was diversity in siting choices, produced cumulative profits that were twice as high as the profits the teams in the other game achieved.

In the discussion that followed, the teams in the game that generated the lower profits realized that they hadn't even considered the competitive consequences of their siting choices. Indeed, they hadn't considered that the competition would erode their profits—they only realized that their profits were less than optimal when they learned of the cumulative profits earned by the teams in the other game. Only when they were presented with the dramatic and unfavorable difference in outcome were they motivated to explore their thinking and the actions that were a product of that thinking. And only at that point did they realize that their own results were profoundly dependent on the decisions the other players made. It was a painful lesson in the need to be mindful of complexity, and it started them down the experiential path of seeing themselves as capable of wading into complexity. All the same, as one of the students remarked, it was a "good thing we weren't playing with real money!"

6. I Give Myself Time to Create a Better Model

Perhaps the single toughest aspect of stance to teach is the element of patience. On this front I have my mother's wise admonition ringing in my ears. Every time she attempted to rein in my impatience—and she did so frequently—she would assert, "Patience is a virtue, seldom found in women—never found in men!"

The only way students learn a patient stance is to experience the unsatisfactory results of not giving themselves enough time. After the HR executive group and the MBA students in the business simulation game systematically reflected on their own thinking, did they suddenly acquire the ability to wade into complexity fearlessly and allow themselves the time to create a better model?

Hardly. But the exercises helped lay the foundation for a stance more like that of an integrative thinker. By exploring their own thinking, they got a taste of complexity. And by understanding the flawed thinking behind the unsatisfactory outcomes they produced, they discovered why it was worth the mental and emotional effort required to accept complexity and take time to forge a creative resolution.

7

A Leap of the Mind

How Integrative Thinkers Connect the Dots

*Give me a lever long enough and a fulcrum on which to place it,
and I shall move the world.*

—Archimedes

ACTUARIES JOKE that they're like accountants, but without the sizzling personality. And at first blush, actuary Taddy Blecher, co-founder of CIDA City Campus, an innovative South African university, seems to fit the stereotype. The gold medal winner in 1990 as the top actuarial science student in the country, he is small and slight and wears the obligatory thick-lensed spectacles. His rumpled clothes and running shoes speak volumes about his fashion sense.

But the stereotype crumbles as soon as he opens his mouth:

When people say "you can't do it," and all the reasons why, we set out to prove that you can, in fact. You can take kids out of the gutter, you can take people off the streets who've had absolutely no opportunities, who come from broken homes, and you can help those people live amazing lives and actually become the fabric of a new society.

These things sound so serious, they sound so impossible to solve.
They are so solvable. They are so solvable! There are infinite numbers
of ways that we can create wealth in sub-Saharan Africa. There are so
many jobs that could be filled.[1]

Audiences give this actuary-turned-social entrepreneur their rapt
attention when he speaks, and they feel a sense of loss when the
words stop. Like souls at a revival meeting presenting themselves
to be saved, listeners walk up to him after his talks to volunteer to
work for the university, officially known as Community and Individual Development Agency City Campus. So maybe Blecher has
a bit too much charisma to fit neatly into the actuarial stereotype.

Building Something from Nothing

Like the other integrative thinkers we've met, Blecher faced a
crisis when his life's work presented him with a set of unacceptable trade-offs. His dilemma concerned the state of education
available for the huge population of young blacks in South Africa
in 1999. The end of apartheid opened new political opportunities
to these young people, but they enjoyed little in the way of economic opportunity. Unemployment among black youth was more
than 40 percent, and they had few opportunities to upgrade their
education—a serious problem in a country where only 6 percent
of the population had a university education at all.

Blecher wanted to offer his young compatriots a chance at an
education and a better life. He had two obvious options for attack-
ing the problem: traditional "contact" education or the newer
option of distance education. "Both of them have got fantastic ad-

vantages," Blecher says, "but they've also got very, very real disadvantages in sub-Saharan Africa." Traditional education was problematic because it had been scaled to the white minority, which traditionally was the only segment of the population eligible to attend university. Of the country's 4.4 million whites (9 percent of a total population of 47 million), 65 percent had a high school education. Only 14 percent of blacks, who made up 75 percent of the population, had an equivalent level of education.

The existing educational infrastructure lacked the capacity to absorb the backlog of young blacks previously denied education.[2] And that was before any considerations of cost. A university education cost more than $5,000 year, a sum far beyond the reach of most black families and more than the government could afford on a scale large enough to make a real difference.

As for distance education, it worked fine in highly developed countries with well-established educational and communications infrastructures. Motivated and well-prepared students with strong social networks could thrive without hands-on guidance from professors. But apartheid had robbed South Africa's black students of a solid educational foundation. They had little in the way of a support network and few role models, because young blacks were almost always the first in their families to go on to post-secondary education. "One's really got to create some sort of third model," Blecher decided.

Blecher set out to bring that third model into being, using technology, ingenuity, and sheer improvisational élan to provide to young blacks the support, coaching, and discipline that contact education had traditionally given young South African whites. His first order of business was to attack the educational cost structure.

Blecher, with his profoundly optimistic stance, didn't view his lack of financial resources as a serious impediment. "It's not that we need more financial resources," he told himself, "we just need to think differently and more creatively and more intelligently, to create everything out of nothing."

The campus building itself, the former downtown Johannesburg headquarters of Investec bank, typifies Blecher's something-from-nothing approach. It was donated to CIDA because its owner deemed it worthless after most tenants fled the violence and urban decay of downtown Johannesburg.[3]

Students themselves help keep costs low. They're in class eight to nine hours a day, and in addition, they cook, clean, and do the university's maintenance and paperwork—in the process learning skills they can apply in their careers. Architecture students help construct the facilities. Agriculture students grow food for the dining hall. Tourism students run a hotel. Classes, which focus exclusively on business and entrepreneurship, are taught pro bono by local executives, and corporations donate computers, books, and equipment.

Such exercises in creative frugality have brought the annual cost of a CIDA education down to about $1,000 per student, a level at which corporations and individual donors can afford to sponsor students. Resources are still scarce, but even the most severe shortages can be overcome by Blecher's boundless ability to make something from nothing. On CIDA's opening day in 1999, Blecher still hadn't received the computers a donor had promised. No matter. He handed each student a photocopy of a keyboard, and they used the photocopies for typing lessons. When the computers finally showed up months later, students were already typing proficiently.

The entire university community is enlisted to weave a social support network out of nothing. Students are required to "adopt" thirty students each from their former high schools and help prepare them for attending CIDA. Within five years after graduation, each graduate is expected to fund a scholarship for one CIDA student. By Blecher's estimate, such outreach efforts have touched six hundred thousand South African youths since the school's founding in 1999.

With only fifteen hundred full-time four-year students, plus an equal number in shorter vocational courses, CIDA is still small. But it has already met Blecher's strategic goal, which he said was to "build a university and then build a whole economy around it and a community around it. It's completely self-sustaining and self-generating because it's generating its own economic activity." And CIDA is well on its way to fulfilling the mission statement Blecher crafted as he imagined what a new-model university could be.

"CIDA's vision," the statement reads, "is to create an advanced, financially focused, state-of-the-art educational site with worldwide acclaim, which produces significant results in every area including: academic, personal development, alumni success, innovation, cost-effectiveness, speed of learning, technology-enriched learning, sport and culture, and societal transformation."

Blecher's work hasn't gone unnoticed. CIDA has won the 2002 Age of Innovation grand prize for the most innovative organization in South Africa, and Blecher has been honored with the World Economic Forum Global Leader for Tomorrow Award (2002) and the Skoll Award for Social Entrepreneurship (2006). But in conversation with him, I sense that the recognition is valuable to him only because it helps spread his vision of an educational system that is rooted in the realities of sub-Saharan Africa.

By now, you can probably detect in Blecher's stance the tell-tale signs of an integrative thinker. Existing models are to his mind just models, each with something useful to offer. But there's a better model just around the corner, and Blecher believes he can find it. The search will carry him deep into complexity and will require him to wait patiently for a better answer to take shape. But he's confident he'll find the answer.

In this chapter, we inquire into the tools Blecher used to create a new model of post-secondary education. I argue he used two of the three most powerful tools at the disposal of integrative thinkers—generative reasoning and causal modeling. I also discuss a third tool, assertive inquiry, and offer aspiring integrative thinkers a few lessons along the way.

Generative Reasoning

The first of the three tools is generative reasoning, a form of reasoning that inquires into what might be rather than what is. Generative reasoning helps build a framework for creative resolutions that is sturdy enough to withstand the rigors of the real world.

Most of us were never taught generative reasoning. Western education emphasizes declarative reasoning, which, as the term suggests, is a cognitive tool for determining the truth or falsity of a given proposition. It operates through deductive and inductive logic, which dominate both education and discourse in the world of business.

Deductive logic—the logic of what should be—is the first mode of reasoning most of us were taught. It entails establishing a framework and then applying the framework to a problem. In biology class, we would have learned that mammals are vertebrates with warm blood that procreate via live birth. When the teacher asked us if bears were mammals, we used deductive logic to test the veracity of the proposition. Do bears come into the world via live births? Check. And they have warm blood? Check. Both conditions are satisfied, ergo, we can declare that bears are mammals.

Now let's use deductive logic to test the proposition that snakes are mammals. Live births? No, snakes lay eggs. Are they warm-blooded? No. Ergo, snakes are not mammals. What about birds? They fit one part of the pattern, being warm-blooded, but not another, because they lay eggs. Thus, birds are not mammals.

The next type of logic most of us learned is inductive—the logic of what is operative—which infers general rules from empirical observation and draws conclusions about what is and isn't true. When we see the sun rising in the east every morning, while never coming up in the west, we establish from a preponderance of data that the sun always rises in the east. That's induction. The technique of market research that many of us learned in business school is another application of inductive reasoning. If we ask questions of a statistically significant sample of consumers, we can draw conclusions from the preponderance of data to understand what they want.

Most of us learned to use ever more sophisticated techniques of deductive and inductive logic as we progressed through formal education, all in service of declarative reasoning—the ability to declare a proposition to be true or false. We received little or no instruction in an equally useful form of reasoning known as modal reasoning. It uses logic to inquire into what could possibly be true.

Integrative thinkers reason about what might be—about models that don't yet exist—to generate a creative resolution.

Modal reasoning makes use of deductive and inductive logic, but it also requires a third form of logic, dubbed abductive logic by Charles Sanders Peirce. He hit on the concept to help him explain the logic that went into what he called "inventive construction of theories."[4] To Peirce, neither deductive nor inductive logic satisfactorily explained how entirely new models came into being. Deductive logic needed a preexisting theory or model on which to base its reasoning. Inductive logic sought to draw inferences from repeated experiences or observations. But invention, Peirce saw, required a logic for making "leaps with your mind."

In essence, abductive logic seeks the best explanation—that is, it attempts to create the best model—in response to novel or interesting data that doesn't fit an extant model. Deductive or inductive logic might prove such a model true or untrue over time, but in the interim, abductive logic generates the best explanation of the data. That's why I call the process of using abductive logic "generative reasoning." This process inquires after what might be, and thus is modal in intent. It employs abductive logic to leap beyond the available data to generate a new model.

Business is fertile ground for abductive logic. Business managers, management theorist Jim March and his colleagues observe, often have only a handful of data points on which to make highly consequential decisions. March posits a business with a poor record of making major marketable discoveries. It wants to increase the return on its innovation investment. But because the firm has a scant history of innovation, the firm's managers don't have nearly enough data points to determine inductively the best model for innovation. And without an established innovation model, it can't use deduction to determine the soundness of a given course.[5] This is just the sort of routine business problem that cries out for the inventive leaps of generative reasoning.

Modal reasoning and abductive logic are not completely untaught in the West. Some design schools teach students to investigate users' needs that have gone unrecognized and invent designs to suit those needs. But nearly all the students learning business or other left-brain subjects (which is to say, highly rational, quantitative, and methodical disciplines) have had no educational exposure to generative reasoning at all.

Where many of their colleagues find generative reasoning to be suspect, integrative thinkers implicitly accept that generative reasoning is both conceptually legitimate and, practically speaking, the only tool suited to the job of fashioning a creative resolution. Generative reasoning facilitates the trial and error that is integral to creative resolution. As integrative thinkers put their resolution through multiple prototypes and iterations, they use generative reasoning—whose raw material, remember, is what does not yet exist—to work back down from resolution to architecture to causality to salience. Large organizations may not recognize generative reasoning as a legitimate mode of inquiry, but they depend on it for lasting competitive advantage.

Much of Blecher's reasoning about CIDA can be best described as generative. Like any observer, he saw that an overwhelming majority of South African blacks were poor, uneducated, and dispirited. But he also saw, as others did not, that young Africans could flourish in the right conditions. Given a helping hand, many escaped their seemingly hopeless circumstances, then extended a hand back to help their communities and make a positive difference in South African society. He saw that other low-income countries such as India and China had made rapid social and economic progress, and he could see no reason why the same couldn't happen in Africa. He had seen South African entrepreneurs create wealth and opportunity where it hadn't existed before. And as befits an integrative thinker, Blecher used abductive reasoning to discover a pattern among these disparate data points.

"It's not through handouts and giving to the poor that poverty is ultimately changed," he concluded. "It's really through teaching people how to create wealth and, through entrepreneurship, really helping people help themselves. What we're doing is not just building a university; what we really have to do is help people reconstruct a reason to live."

Blecher didn't actually have sufficient data either to make that vision his purpose in life or to see CIDA as the means of achieving it. He couldn't prove it in advance or deduce or induce it from the existing theories or data. It required him to make leaps in his mind to reason about what might be. Let's examine what that reasoning looks like in practice.

The Art and Science of Generative Reasoning

My colleagues and I at Rotman try to teach MBA students and executives to reason generatively. We teach them how to seek insights that don't fit neatly into the existing models. Then we ask them to proceed from those insights to visualize new models. We also teach them to how to prototype and refine their mental models, gathering additional data with each iteration. Many students find it scary, and somewhat transgressive, to flex their abductive logic muscles, having been taught to see deductive and inductive logic as the only legitimate forms of reasoning. It's always a pleasure to see the light come on as they realize that generative reasoning does not destroy life as we know it. To the contrary—it opens the door to new possibilities.

When we teach executive groups, we use the dilemmas they face in their current businesses as the modeling challenge. One group of executives that came through recently was from a hair-care business that wanted to increase its share of the styling-products market. One evening, we arranged for them to visit a hair salon and watch a group of women get their hair styled. The next morning, the executives interviewed the women in detail.

The aim of the exercise was to give the executives a deeper understanding of how users felt about the styling experience. We emphasized to the executives that we didn't want them to gather a statistically significant sample but to seek a deeper understanding of the end users of their products. Then we asked them to use that understanding to imagine new ways to meet the needs of the women in the salon. In other words, we asked them to infer backward from their understanding to the "best explanation"—in this case, a product that would meet their customers' needs better than anything yet on the market. We worked with them to prototype and refine their new offerings until they were ready to be tested on the target customers—the ladies in the salon.

MBA students at Rotman hone their abductive reasoning skills on challenges proposed by corporations or nonprofits. Just as the hair-care executives did, the MBA students work through a series of exercises aimed initially at gaining a deeper understanding of the users of a particular product or service. Then we ask them to visualize new ways of serving those users and mentally work their way through a series of prototypes of the new product or service.

Both MBA students and seasoned executives often find these exercises unsettling. They share certainties about the world and about the deductive and inductive logics that confirm their certainties. It makes them uneasy to deliberately seek out data that unsettles their certainties. As they gain practice with the mental exercises, though, they grow less defensive when faced with disconfirming data and more eager to make something new of the novel and different data they've uncovered. What had been a threat becomes an exhilarating form of play.

Causal Modeling

The second tool of integrative thinkers, also illustrated by Blecher, is causal modeling. Sophisticated causal modeling is a crucial underpinning for causality and architecture, the middle two steps of the integrative thinking process. Recall that in the causality step, the thinker must consider nonlinear and multidirectional causal links between salient variables. In the architecture step, the thinker must keep the whole interlocking structure of causal relationships in mind while working on the individual parts of a solution.

To build sophisticated models, we need to consciously acquire tools. We don't have to do that to build basic models. After all, we're natural model builders, with a factory setting biased in favor of shaping the fabric of our experiences into mental models. "You never have the choice of 'let's model or not,'" says John

Sterman, a professor at MIT Sloan School of Management and a leading thinker in system dynamics. "It's only a question of which model. And most of the time, the models that you're operating from are ones that you're not even aware that you're using."[6] Integrative thinkers differ from the rest of us in being more conscious about the tools they choose to use to model.

Two forms of causation are important to causal modeling. The first is material causation, which says that under a certain set of conditions, x causes y to happen: If we price our product 10 percent below our competitors' price (x), our market share (y) will rise.

The second form of causation we need to know about is teleological causation, which asks, what is the purpose of y, or why do we want y to happen? Let's say you're a CEO who wants to increase market share so your company can increase scale and reap the resulting economies. For the causal modeler, material causation and teleological causation connect the way things are to their desired end-state. Material causation is how we know that if we press this button, we shut down the nuclear reactor. Teleological causation is the process by which we understand that if we want to shut down the reactor, we press the button. When the desire to shut down the reactor causes us to press the button, we're enlisting the material to achieve the teleological. We aim to change the present state (a hot reactor) into a desired end-state (a cool one), and we do so by following a known chain of material causation.

For Blecher, the existing state was of disadvantaged, disempowered black youth who had neither hope nor opportunity. His desired end-state was that they would have self-esteem and capability. His task as an integrative thinker was to build a causal model to get from the current state to the desired end-state.

The material causation that he envisioned was to give the students the tools they needed to understand their world better and contribute to it. "This process really builds a tremendous sense of ownership in the students and a sense of self-belief," Blecher explains. But this material causation requires a narrow and specific set of conditions to be operative. "It requires," he says, "a very special kind of education that is enormously loving, enormously holistic, and really does give the students the opportunity to completely change the way they feel about themselves."

Blecher built a concrete causal model that informed his actions in designing CIDA. His challenge as an integrative thinker imagining what might be was to visualize the causal relationships in enough depth and detail that his vision would hold up in the real world. When facing this challenge, certain tools, known as system dynamics, can improve the causal modeling.

System dynamics is a theory of mapping the activity of complex systems that Jay Forrester of MIT developed in the early 1960s. He brought the tool set from the engineering domain and applied it to the business world.[7] System dynamics holds that the results of our decisions are so often disappointing because we overlook important causal relationships, or because we misread causal relationships, usually by assuming them to be linear and unidirectional when they are in fact nonlinear and multidirectional.

A primary focus of system dynamics is one sort of causal relationship: multidirectional feedback loops that accelerate relationships between variables. Here's an example: hotel developers are often dismayed to discover that when they open a hotel in a market that supports high room rates, those rates often fall because the new hotel increases local capacity. The usual managerial response is to cut costs and prices, but that step often hurts the hotel's premium image, and thus its occupancy and profitability. Another round of cost- and price-cutting ensues, doing further damage to occupancy and profitability. Repeat, with accelerating frequency, until bankruptcy.

System dynamics experts call that an accelerating feedback loop. A person could not model the dynamic accurately or intelligently without an ability to imagine nonlinear, multidirectional causal relationships.

System dynamics tools help integrative thinkers consider complex causal loops in creating their models and help them build models in which the whole is viewed together rather than split into discrete components. In fact, in system dynamics, the whole *must* be held in mind to capture and understand all the relevant causal feedback loops.

Such feedback loops are built into Blecher's model for CIDA. His view of a self-sustaining, self-generating university community, surrounded and nourished by student-led businesses, assumes feedback loops between education and commerce. Another feedback loop forms when students adopt thirty high school students from their home communities. And Blecher's preferred practice of creating something out of nothing is a third accelerating feedback loop, in which a handful of resources begets greater resources, which in turn beget ever-greater resources. The man makes a mean pot of stone soup.

Causal model building and generative reasoning combine to form one of the most potent tools in the integrative thinker's kit. Generative reasoning seeks to build new models that take into account data that doesn't comport with the current models available. A tool for forming such models is what George Lakoff and Mark Johnson call "radial metaphors," by which one devises a metaphor and builds a model around that metaphor.[8] For example, people commonly use a few different metaphors to describe a business organization. The metaphor might be that of a sports team, in which the employees are the players, business competition is a game, business etiquette and business ethics are the rules of the game, and customers are the fans. Another common metaphor is that of the family. Senior executives are parents, employees are children, the task of the organization is to nurture, the resources of the organization are love and affection, and resource allocation is based on suitability of behavior. Other metaphors around which a structure takes shape are the organization as army, the organization as market, and the organization as ecosystem.

The radial metaphor tool helps integrative thinkers in two ways. First, it helps thinkers conceive of the situation at hand in a way that's conducive to creating a new model. In that sense, the radial metaphor is one of those tools of efficiency discussed in the first half of the book.

The radial metaphor also helps with the cognitive heavy lifting of keeping a coherent whole in mind while honing the individual parts. That skill is critical to integrative thinking, and the radial metaphor can be an invaluable help.

Blecher's radial metaphor when building the CIDA model was the organization as family. CIDA is the nurturing and loving parent and the students are the children who thrive on the parent's love. Blecher is quite explicit about the role love and affection play in his vision of education. But love and discipline go hand in hand. Students must obey CIDA's many rules if they want to continue to receive the school's love and nurturing.

Blecher's causal modeling of CIDA can be seen at three levels. At the basic level, there's the combination of teleological and material modeling (young people can gain the desired hope and self-worth through education). At the next level, Blecher modeled a dynamic system that takes advantage of the feedback effects between happy, motivated, and successful students and the communities in which they live, work, and socialize. At the third level is that radial metaphor of the CIDA organization as a family.

Working on these three causal levels, Blecher used insights that had eluded other observers to build an entirely new model to resolve the trade-offs he faced. The three levels of modeling enabled him to see the basic causal relationships between relevant variables, the more sophisticated relationships, and finally, to hold the whole picture in his mind while working on the individual pieces.

At Rotman, we give students practice at all three levels of causal modeling. The simplest practice is to ask students to reverse engineer their own models. We ask them to pick a belief (better grades help get a better job) or practice (calling team meetings every Friday morning) and break down the causal reasoning that underlies the belief or practice. This helps them recognize how they're already using causal modeling without realizing it, and shows how the modeling might improved by being more explicit about it.

We then graduate to interviewing another person to understand the causal modeling that underlies a particular belief or practice. This exercise entails speculating on the logic another person follows to arrive at a particular conclusion, and many students find it challenging. One student interviewed her female counterpart about her decision to break off an engagement with only weeks to go until the wedding. The interviewer's first attempt at imagining her counterpart's causal model focused on the aspects that were easy to describe in practical, utilitarian terms. One such aspect was that their careers weren't suited for one another. Another was that they wanted to work in different cities.

But in discussing this model with her interview subject, our interviewer soon understood that it didn't offer a complete or convincing account of the problem. It failed to take into account powerful emotional forces that played at least as large a role in the decision to break off the engagement as any practical concerns.

The most important takeaway from these interview sessions is that it's extremely difficult to build a causal model that adequately takes account of human beings and their wishes and dreams. It taxes students' abilities to take a wide view of what's salient, to perceive complex causal relationships, and to hold the whole in mind while drilling down on a particular part.

The faculty's goals in these exercises are threefold. First, we want students to see themselves as thinkers capable of conscious causal modeling. We want them to understand that their modeling gains power and effectiveness when they're conscious and explicit about it. And we want them to practice using techniques such as system dynamics and radial metaphors to build sophisticated causal models.

Assertive Inquiry

The third important tool for the integrative thinker is assertive inquiry. Integrative thinkers use it to explore opposing models, and in particular, models that oppose their own.

When we interact with other people on the basis of a particular mental model, we usually try to defend that model against any challenges. Our energy goes into explaining our model to others and defending it from criticism. Parrying critiques of our model gives us a deeper understanding of it, but it teaches us nothing about the models other people hold in their heads. In fact, the defensive stance helps ensure that we never learn anything about models that might oppose our own. And that keeps us from finding clues that might lead to a creative resolution should our mental model come into conflict with someone else's mental model.

The antidote to advocacy is inquiry, which produces meaningful dialogue. When you use assertive inquiry to investigate someone else's mental model, you find saliencies that wouldn't have occurred to you and causal relationships you didn't perceive. You may not want to adopt the mental model as your own, but even the least compelling model can provide clues to saliencies or causal relationships that will generate a creative resolution.

Assertive inquiry's intent isn't argumentative, and its method isn't to ask leading questions ("don't you think that . . . ?") or discourage challenge ("wouldn't you agree that that . . . ?"). Assertive inquiry involves a sincere search for another's views ("could you please help me understand how you came to believe that?") and tries to fill in gaps of understanding ("could you clarify that point for me with an illustration or example?"). It seeks common ground between conflicting models ("how does what you are saying overlap, if at all, with what I suggested?").

Assertive inquiry isn't a form of challenge, but it is pointed. It explicitly seeks to explore the underpinnings of your own model and that of another person. Its aim is to learn about the salient data and causal maps baked into another person's model, then use the insight gained to fashion a creative resolution of the conflict between that person's model and your own.

Assertive inquiry promotes generative reasoning and causal modeling. It enables generative reasoning by breaking down conflicting models into pieces that can be recombined into something better than either of the two models that are in conflict. And assertive inquiry produces more robust causal modeling by enlisting more minds to explore and map the material and teleological links that undergird the conflicting models.

My colleagues and I try to imbue our students with a similar curiosity about other people's mental models. Many aren't eager to learn. To them, clashing models have always meant only conflict, hurt feelings, and misunderstanding. Our task is to help them come away from an episode of clashing models feeling that they have made something positive of the clash and contributed to a valuable resolution.

We try to teach students how to engage in productive dialogue in the face of clashing models, and the vehicle we use for teaching it is the "personal case." I have adopted the technique from the methods and theories of Chris Argyris, a professor emeritus at Harvard Business School and a leading theorist of organizational learning.[9] We ask each class participant to recall an encounter with another person that involved a clash of views or positions. This encounter, moreover, had to end badly, in egocentric terms. That is, the outcome had to be less favorable than the one the student sought at the outset of the interaction. If it is only a failure in the minds of others, the student can distance himself or herself from the failure (i.e., I succeeded but they thought it was a failure), and in doing so, lessen the learning.

We ask participants to explain in a paragraph or two the purpose of the failed encounter, and then in another paragraph or two explain what they hoped the interaction would accomplish, and how. Then we ask them to record, as best they can recall, the actual conversation during the interaction, and present it as dialogue in a play.

We ask that they display the dialogue on the right half of the page. On the left half, we ask them to provide a sort of running commentary on the dialogue, made up of what they thought and felt but did not say. Finally, we ask them to write a paragraph or two of reflection on the outcome of the interaction.

We discuss each case in small groups for approximately one hour. The purpose is to help class participants diagnose what went wrong in the interaction, how they inadvertently contributed to an outcome that they didn't like, and how they could have dealt more productively with model clash. At the end of the exercise, we want participants to better understand how they built from directly observable data to higher-order conclusions, and how that sequence might have ended in a productive resolution instead of unproductive conflict. Let's now look at the actual case of an MBA student, with names and identifying context disguised (see "A Failure to Communicate").

A Failure to Communicate

The author of the following personal case, MBA student Philip, described his part in bringing about a very painful clash. When each participant—including Philip—clung tenaciously to his own model, the outcome bore no relation to the ending Philip had hoped to achieve.

Purpose of the Encounter

Immediately after graduating with my undergraduate degree, I started up a small Internet consulting company with two friends who were in similar situations. The time of the following encounter was a little over one year after we started the company. We had done well, in the sense that the company made enough money for us all to live on. However, we all felt as though the company had stagnated over the past few months, that our initial momentum to "be wildly successful" had given way to running the company merely to meet our lifestyle needs, which were very modest.

We attributed this stagnation to the fact that we hadn't formally divided up ownership of the company. It was registered as a sole proprietorship in the name of Dennis, one of the three of us. With the company being his sole personal liability, he was unwilling to take the kinds of risky/big moves that Aaron and I were interested in taking to grow the company. Conversely, while Aaron and I had worked very hard initially to build a foundation for the company, we were now unwilling to "give our all" to the company, bringing it to the next level, before we knew that we were going to have an equity stake in any success we might help create.

The purpose of the encounter was to establish the ownership percentages of the company so that we could go forward with it.

What I Wanted to Accomplish and How I Hoped to Do So

I recognized that Dennis was a phenomenally talented guy who took the initial step to found the company, and as a result he could be "first among equals" once ownership shares were formally established. However, I saw the company essentially as a venture of equals and I wanted the ownership shares to reflect this—say, 40/30/30 for Dennis, Aaron, and me (or at least something very close to this).

I hoped to achieve this outcome by explaining my reasoning and viewpoint along these lines. I thought that skills and time commitment to date of all three of us was prima facie evidence that we all essentially were equals, and that unless we codified this, the company couldn't move forward.

What I thought and felt but did not say	What we actually said and did
	Me: I guess the fundamental question we have to address is which model of equity division are we going to approach: one where there is a distinct difference between one of us versus the other two, or one where we're all generally equal, but with variations that reflect different skills or other contributions?
Dennis, yes, you're talented, but get a hold of yourself —you're not that much more talented. Besides, I'm the one who held this company together while you finished your last year of school.	*Dennis:* I feel as though my contributions to date warrant a fundamentally different level of control from the two of you. Also, as it stands right now, I have 100 percent control over the company. Why on earth would I move myself from the current situation, where I have control, to one where I don't? What if the two of you decide to gang up on me?

What I thought and felt but did not say	What we actually said and did
	Me: As far as your observation regarding relative contribution to date goes, I disagree. I think we've all given a hell of a lot to the company, with no one of us head and shoulders above the others. Regarding your observation about giving up control, put yourself in our shoes—that's the situation that Aaron and I are in right now, only worse! It only takes one of you to "gang up" on the two of us!
You always have felt as though you're some kind of "special case," haven't you? I knew you were a control freak, but now I'm beginning to see how much of one you are.	*Dennis:* I am unmoved by your arguments. Since I'm the boss currently, my own opinion regarding worthiness wins. And whatever reasons you and Aaron had for accepting the current situation are your own —I don't feel as though they apply to me.
	Me: While I can't speak for Aaron, I can say that the reason why I've been willing for you to be the 100 percent owner to date has been that, up until now, it really hasn't been an issue of much practical importance.

What I thought and felt but did not say	What we actually said and did
	Me: We're on the cusp of growing the company, taking on much more risk and hopefully getting much more reward than has been the case in the past. If there's big reward to be had, I want my share. But I think the fundamental issue is what is going to happen next for this company. I feel my talents are needed for this company to move to the next level, and I don't plan on giving them away without getting a level of equity acceptable to me as a result.
Dennis, you moron! Do you really think that? Is this just a negotiation ploy, or has your ego detached you that much from reality? Aaron, you moron! Don't you realize that I'm fighting for you, too? Oh, I get it. You're just being a weasel because you're worried about paying your rent next month. You've got zero guts!	*Dennis:* I disagree—I think this company can grow without the kind of equity division that you describe, one where I lose control. *Aaron:* I think it's clear now that Dennis isn't going to move from his position. That's okay with me. If that's the way he wants to play it, then that's the way it will be.

What I thought and felt but did not say	What we actually said and did
	Me: With this outcome, I don't believe that this company has a long-term future, and so I have to look to my own best interests to see if something else out there is going to work out better for me.

Concerns

Within a month after this meeting, I had accepted a job at a large IT company in another city. Dennis and Aaron continued the Internet consulting business. The business shut down three years later when Dennis went to business school for an MBA and Aaron decided not to continue the business so he could pursue other creative interests. The client list was sold and both Dennis and Aaron profited from this. In the three years the business didn't grow to a size we originally envisioned, but a few other employees were brought in under various arrangements.

My concern is this: While I don't generally expect anything from people other than self-interest, is there any way that I could have approached this situation to have helped the other people involved to appreciate that my position was probably the course of enlightened self-interest? After all, while Dennis won (or at least kept) 100 percent control, 100 percent of not much is still not much. What could I do in the face of this way of thinking? Or am I thinking about this all wrong even now?

It is easy to see how this interaction would reinforce Philip's aversion to model clash. An interaction like the one he recounted isn't likely to instill confidence in achieving a constructive resolution of clashing models.

According to Philip, Steve prevailed in this conflict by insisting that he didn't find the situation unsatisfactory and saw no need for change. "What could I do," Philip asked plaintively, "in the face of this way of thinking?"

The question may have been rhetorical, but there is an answer: try something other than pure advocacy in the face of an opposing model. Note that neither Philip nor Dennis inquires into the other man's model (Dennis's two rhetorical questions—"Why on earth would I move myself from the current situation, where I have control, to one where I don't?" and "What if the two of you decide to gang up on me?"—are aimed at shutting down inquiry, not opening it up). Each repeatedly advocates the merits of his own model and shows little or no interest in the logic of the opposing model.

Both Philip and Dennis, being proud products of Western education, are highly skilled advocates. Each advocates his model vigorously and thoroughly and sees his primary task as gaining the other's acceptance of his model. In the face of nonacceptance, each advocates more forcefully or refutes what he understands to be the other's model. They signal to one another that each is completely uninterested in understanding the concerns, assumptions, and salient data that inform the other man's thinking.

The dialogue Philip recreates is notable for its increasing emotional heat. Because Philip shares his unspoken thoughts with us, we can see his characterization of Dennis morph from "talent" to "control freak" to "moron" in the space of several minutes. The anger seeps over to the right side of the dialogue box in more inflammatory language ("I don't plan on giving them away") and more extreme positions ("so I have to look to my own best interests"). Advocacy fuels the responses that fuel the anger, which fuels more advocacy and more anger, in an accelerating cycle with no good end.

Because neither man is actively engaged in learning more about the other's thinking, no creative resolution of their conflict is possible. A creative resolution requires one or the other party in the dialogue to recognize additional salient data and perceive more or different causal relationships. Repeated and intensifying advocacy does not broaden salience, make causality more sophisticated, or facilitate holistic architecture. It crowds out the conditions necessary for creative resolution.

Assertive inquiry is the tool needed to break the impasse. The conversation would have gone much differently if Dennis could have responded to Philip's opening statement with something like this: "I understand that you feel that your share of the economic return of the business is too low. Have you given any thought to the issue of managerial control? Do you feel you have too little managerial control over the business, or is your interest primarily financial?" Likewise, Philip could have answered Dennis's initial response with something like this: "I understand that managerial control is important to you. I have two questions. First, are you agreeing that my stake in the economic return is too low, or am I misinterpreting you? And second, could you tell me more about your concerns about sharing control with Aaron and me?" Both responses combine advocacy—embedded in the restatement of the other's point—with an assertive inquiry into the salient data and causal assumptions that underlie Dennis's model.

This alternative inquiry is valuable in several respects. It opens up a cornucopia of new salient data and causal links that can be mined for creative resolutions. It also paves the way for continued productive dialogue by signaling a genuine interest in Dennis's views, though they conflict with Philip's own. And it invites Dennis to inquire into Philip's thinking, supplying additional energy for crafting a creative resolution.

It doesn't actually take a great deal of work to find a creative resolution to the present conflict. Philip's primary concern is to increase his financial return from the business. Dennis wants to retain managerial control. Those objectives need not be in irreconcilable conflict. A dual-class share structure that left Dennis with majority voting control would satisfy his concerns and still enhance Philip's financial equity in the business. If both weren't so focused on defending the validity of their own models, they could see their way through to this resolution fairly easily.

Personal cases help class participants see that the tool of assertive inquiry can get them past the dead end of unadulterated advocacy. By twinning advocacy with inquiry, participants learn how to give their opposable minds a chance to produce a constructive solution out of what seemed at first to be a conflict with no exit. Tools such as assertive inquiry allow integrative thinkers to give their stances force in the world. And experience, as we shall see in the next and final chapter, enables integrative thinkers to wield those tools with precision, accuracy, and lasting impact.

8

A Wealth of Experience

Using the Past, Inventing the Future

I am always doing that which I can not do,
in order that I may learn how to do it.

—Pablo Picasso

AS I BROUGHT TO A CLOSE my eight-hour interview with A.G. Lafley, I was deeply struck with the power of well-considered and well-leveraged experiences.[1] In walking through thirty-three years of decision-making experience with him, from running a U.S. Navy retail operation to running P&G since 2000, I came to appreciate how Lafley processed and capitalized on his experiences to become a consummate integrative thinker. The most striking aspect was how he used his experiences both to deepen his mastery and nurture his originality, rather than focusing on one at the expense of the other.

Lafley's managerial career started in 1972, while he was still in the Navy. Through the sort of fluke that military bureaucracies are famous for, Lafley found himself running the Navy Exchange—the service's term for the retail stores that service its bases around the world—at the giant Atsugi Naval Base, just south of Tokyo.

In quick succession after Lafley arrived at the exchange, the base manager had a heart attack and the assistant manager who succeeded him was transferred to a larger exchange in the United States. Suddenly, the self-described "twenty-four-year-old kid" with "zero" business knowledge or experience was managing a retail operation that served the base's population of several thousand, as well as any U.S. military personnel in the greater Tokyo area who had the inclination to shop there.

Although he lacked tools or experiences, the young Lafley, with his optimistic stance, sought to build the exchange's business. He studied his customers intensively, seeking to understand who they were and why they were buying. He learned that when ships' crews came to Tokyo on leave, they wanted to buy cameras and stereo equipment but could be talked into buying perfume on their way out. He understood that the families living on the base shopped for necessities first, luxuries second. The visitors were just the opposite.

Lafley also realized that since customers had to show their military identification card to shop at the exchange, he could collect data on which customer populations were buying what goods at what prices and adjust his assortment and pricing accordingly. He recalled with some glee that "we just mined the hell out of the data," which previously wasn't even collected.

Only because Lafley wanted to deepen his mastery of retailing did he accumulate these particular experiences. He systematically collected and mined data so that he could structure and plan his business operation to produce the outcome he sought. When he ran a price promotion, he wanted to be able to predict the effect on sales. When the crew of an aircraft carrier came in for shore leave, he wanted to have the right merchandise in the store for that segment of the customer base. His repeated experiences in structuring, focusing, and planning produced a deep understanding of the context in which his business operated and a high level of effectiveness in producing desired outcomes. In other words, he consciously accumulated experiences that cultivated mastery.

While Lafley planned, organized, and crunched his data to deepen his mastery, he also worked to build his capacity for producing novel outcomes. This originality often expressed itself in Lafley's merchandising decisions.

Most of his store's inventory was the standard assortment of American brands that would be found in every exchange around the world. But exchange managers were allowed to stock a small amount of locally sourced merchandise. Most managers in Lafley's position would have defined "local" as the region around Tokyo. But Lafley interpreted "local" to include most of the Far East. He tells of getting to know pilots who sometimes flew cargo runs to Saigon, returning to the base in empty planes. He persuaded the pilots to fly back with a hold full of ceramic elephants from a factory he knew of in Vietnam.

Lafley circulated flyers around the base advertising the elephants and set them up for display on a football field next to the exchange. The morning the elephants went on sale, customers started lining up two hours before the exchange opened, and they surged onto the lot the moment they were allowed through the ropes. Within minutes, Lafley was fresh out of elephants. "It was unbelievable," he recalls with a wry chuckle, "People were running and diving. It was nuts!"

Another time, Lafley got word from a fellow exchange manager that fuel prices were about to skyrocket because of the first OPEC oil price hike in 1973. In response, Lafley commandeered every mothballed fuel storage tank in the base's tank farm, hired members of the engineering corps to clean the sludge out of the tanks in exchange for free beer, and bought every gallon of fuel he could get his hands on. When gas prices went up, he was able to sell fuel at below-market rates for several months, driving up the exchange's customer traffic. He describes that particular adventure as "seize the day stuff."

Those and other experiences honed the edge of Lafley's originality. To make the most of the opportunities before him, Lafley needed to be spontaneous, flexible, and open, willing to experiment and respond quickly to transient opportunities. The ever-shifting customer mix and fast-moving retail environment gave him plenty of practice and strengthened his ability to engage in original thought and action.

Spontaneity, experimentation, flexibility, and openness aren't terribly rare qualities in and of themselves. But it's the mark of an integrative thinker to nurture those markers of originality while at the same time deepening mastery, whose markers—organization, planning, focus, and repetition—are originality's seeming opposite. From his first days as a manager, Lafley was consciously accumulating experiences that strengthened both capabilities—originality *and* mastery, not the one at the expense of the other.

His experiences running the exchange reinforced a key part of his stance—his view of himself as a problem-solving business manager—and convinced him that he needed to upgrade his tools if he was going to continue to progress. The upgrade process started at Harvard Business School and continued when he joined P&G after graduating in 1977. Starting as an assistant brand manager on Joy dish detergent, Lafley spent sixteen years working his way through Tide, Cheer, Downy, Bounce, and the rest of P&G's laundry and cleaning products business, rising to president of the division, P&G's biggest and most profitable.

Through this period, Lafley continued to accumulate experiences that strengthened both ends of the mastery–originality continuum. In particular, he continued to deepen his understanding of consumer behavior, a process begun at the Navy Exchange. The depth of that understanding strengthened his hand during an internal battle in 1984 over the naming of the new liquid version of Tide laundry detergent.

Usually, when P&G developed a substantial innovation of an existing product, the new product got a new and entirely different name. For example, when P&G came up with a new way to clean hard surfaces, it also came up with a new brand name, Swiffer, rather than use the brand name of its leading hard surface cleaner, Mr. Clean. So organizational precedent was firmly on the side of giving the liquid detergent a new name.

Lafley saw good reason for breaking precedent. "We had convinced ourselves that powder Tide was for particulate soil remover and liquid detergent was for greasy, oily food removal," he says. But Lafley had done enough loads of laundry at home to know that the distinction was meaningful only to the scientists who developed P&G's detergent formula. "The issue was," Lafley says, "how does the consumer see it?" The consumer saw the detergent as the same old reliable Tide in a convenient new form. Why not, then, call the product liquid Tide?

The logic of Lafley's argument prevailed, and thus, liquid Tide arrived in the marketplace. Within twenty years, the U.S. market for liquid detergent was more than three times the size of the powdered detergent market, and liquid and powdered Tide had claimed more than four times the share of the next biggest brand. Had the liquid detergent been branded under a separate name, it's not likely that Tide would be an immediately recognizable brand, a sixty-year-old mainstay towering over an array of brands with twenty or fewer years on the shelves.

Lafley's mastery helped him make the right call on liquid Tide. His originality came into play when he faced another big decision about packaged laundry soap. In 1993, P&G's R&D folks had devised a way to compact the big fluffy granules of powdered detergent into a form that was less than half the volume. Boxes of the detergent would take up half the space on store shelves and in shopping carts, as well as in the laundry room.

As is its time-honored practice, P&G subjected the new detergent to its usual extensive consumer testing. To nearly everyone's surprise, including Lafley's, tests showed that consumers did not exhibit a strong preference for compact detergent, despite advantages that seemed obvious to Lafley and his colleagues.

The findings placed the product's future in jeopardy. P&G customarily would not launch a new product unless a rigorous quantitative consumer test had deemed it a clear winner over the product it was meant to replace. For a master of consumer understanding like Lafley, the test data should have doomed compact detergents.

But that verdict didn't sit right with Lafley. Everything in P&G's carefully planned and structured experience argued against launching a compact detergent brand. With his carefully nurtured capacity for originality, though, Lafley focused on what was potentially unique about the situation that might call for a novel response from P&G. He saw that unlike the majority of product upgrades, this one had the potential for massive cost savings for retailers. The dramatically smaller boxes would take up half the space in warehouses and on store shelves for the same dollar of sales, resulting in huge cost efficiencies for the retailers. So retailers would love the product, whatever consumers might think of it. And P&G's manufacturing and logistics operations would reap the same cost benefits as the retailers.

But what about the consumers? The quantitative research showed that compact detergent wasn't a clear winner with them, but neither was it an obvious loser. The data worked out to a wash, which under most circumstances would put the kibosh on a product launch. But Lafley decided to dive into the voluntary comments that some of the consumers added to their quantitative research forms. The voluntaries were not statistically significant and ordinarily carried little weight in P&G's deliberations. But to those who knew how to read them, they afforded a much deeper insight into consumers' sentiments than quantitative answers allowed.

Lafley took many evening and weekend hours to pore over more than four hundred handwritten voluntaries. He came to the conclusion that while consumers weren't wildly enthusiastic about compact detergents, few were actively hostile to the idea. In fact, more than 80 percent of the voluntaries cited at least one positive thing about compact detergent.

Lafley totted up the data points. Retailers saw compact detergent as a big win, and so did P&G manufacturing. Consumers were

neutral at worse. So despite the lack of conclusive consumer evidence, Lafley argued for converting all powdered detergents to
compact. It was a massive undertaking that required an appropri-
ation of $250 million of corporate funds, by far the biggest single
investment Lafley had ever advocated.

It turned out to be a big win for P&G. "We ran and we won
the race," Lafley says. "It was huge, absolutely huge." So was the
risk Lafley took in championing it. Had it not worked out, Lafley
could have been fired. But his accumulated mastery and originality gave him the confidence to take the risk. Had Lafley cultivated
only his mastery, the results of the consumer research would have
convinced him not to order the conversion. But while Lafley has
the highest regard for quantitative research, for which P&G is
justly famous, but he doesn't let the data do his deciding for him.
"I trust judgment," he says. "Research is an aid to judgment."

Originality alone would not have supplied a basis for the decision, either. Lafley had to marshal all his accumulated mastery to
understand what the voluntaries meant, how the retailers would
react, and what the impact would be on P&G's manufacturing
and distribution. Without that mastery, Lafley's originality would
not have withstood the rigors of the real world.

Lafley's success in packaged soap earned him a 1994 promotion
to president of P&G's Asia-Pacific region. He headed back to
Japan, where he'd served his apprenticeship in management and
retailing. He had amassed years of experience as a P&G executive,
bringing his mastery and originality to bear on opportunities and
problems. Through experience, Lafley had also become highly
skilled with the tools of consumer understanding and competitive
strategy. As his capacities expanded, they reinforced his stance as

an executive able to convert challenges, complexities, and contradictions into creative resolutions.

Japan presented Lafley with many opportunities to put his mastery and originality to work. Before he arrived as regional president, P&G's experience in Japan had been something of a disappointment. In many business lines it was second- or third-ranked, an unfamiliar spot for a company that dominated its home market in the United States.

In Japan, Lafley exercised his mastery to establish marketing and selling discipline and build the P&G business in an orderly process. At the same time, he gave his originality a workout. When the company launched concentrated Joy dish liquid against the twin dominant Japanese players, each with over 40 percent of the market, the convention in the marketplace was to sell dish soap in large bottles of relatively diluted soap. P&G had figured out how to concentrate about three times the amount of soap into the same volume, allowing the product to be packaged in much more compact bottles. In the previous couple of years, P&G had conducted major launches in the dish cleaning category in the United Kingdom and Germany and both had failed quite miserably against the entrenched home-country competitors, so Lafley had to be wary.

Lafley realized that innovative tactics were called for if concentrated Joy was going to mount a serious challenge to the entrenched market leaders in Japan. P&G positioned the detergent as a superior grease-remover with advertising copy featuring a well-known Japanese comedian conducting a "doorstep challenge" with his bottle of Joy. More surprising was the new product's price. Lafley dispensed with the usual low introductory price and priced Joy concentrate above the two leading brands, on the theory that a premium price signaled a premium product. And instead of launching a line of various sizes and fragrances, Lafley introduced a single item. That focused consumers' attention and allowed the retailers to sell in high volumes using relatively little shelf space.

Lafley reckoned the smartest strategy for the two leading brands would be to promote its regular-strength lineup heavily. That would encourage consumers to reject the whole category of concentrated dish liquid before P&G could establish it. Instead, both competitors appeared to panic, quickly bringing a concentrate to market and promoting it heavily. In effect, both were doing P&G's work by endorsing the idea the concentrate was a better product. That could only help Joy, the first product to market in the category. Lafley admitted his audacious gambit was "a crapshoot because if both had been smarter, if they had picked the right defense, they could have stopped us. But they didn't." As a result, Joy achieved leading market share in the category; a position it has defended since.

Lafley's approach to decision making always takes advantage of mastery, whether his own or another's. "I like experts and masters," he says. "They are invaluable—the proxy for experience that I don't have personally." But mastery in no way diminishes his commitment to originality. After his promotion to CEO in 2000, he engineered a significant overhaul of P&G's culture to make attention to design a core value, championed the Connect & Develop initiative discussed earlier, dramatically expanded P&G's participation in the beauty care business, and made the biggest acquisition in P&G history, the $53 billion purchase of Gillette.[2] "I am quite comfortable with taking risks," Lafley admits.

The first thirty-three years of A. G. Lafley's managerial career teach us several lessons about experiences. The first is that stance and tools influence experiences. Experiences, in turn, influence tools and stance. Experiences can deepen mastery and nurture originality, and those that combine to deepen mastery and nurture originality are the most powerful in enhancing integrative thinking capacity. Let's now take a closer look at those lessons.

How Stance and Tools Influence Experiences

We have an inclination to accumulate experiences that reinforce the stance and tools we start with. That's because stance guides the acquisition of tools, and tools guide the sort of experiences we have. So people who believe that existing models are identical to reality and fear opposing models aren't likely to believe that better models exist. Having a low tolerance for multiple models, they'll be impatient to choose an available model, whatever its shortcomings. They will use only inductive and deductive reasoning, will build highly simplified models, and will advocate their own point of view rather than dispassionately consider multiple points of view. The experiences they gather will tend to reinforce their initial stance and suggest to them that they have all the tools that they need.

In stark contrast, people like Lafley believe existing models are just the best anyone has come up with to date and relish opposing models. Not only do they think a better model is waiting to be found, they think they will find it, by wading into complexity and staying patient. They will use generative reasoning, causal modeling, and assertive inquiry. The experience they gain building new models will reinforce their initial stance, and the skill and sensitivity with which they deploy integrative thinking tools will increase.

Even as an inexperienced Navy officer, Lafley did not accept the existing models for how to run an exchange. From the outset of his managerial career, his stance was that better models could be created. He was happy to wade into complexity to find out how to serve his customers better, how to find unique merchandise, and how to compete with other exchanges and win.

His stance caused him to accumulate experiences that raised his skills. As he added to his understanding of customers, he improved his chances of pulling off merchandising coups like the ceramic elephants. Had he accepted the conventional model of how to run an exchange, he would not have accumulated any of those rich learning experiences that strengthened his personal knowledge system.

How Experiences Influence Stance and Tools

Lafley's experiences taught him both that he liked business and that he needed more sophisticated tools to guide him. His performance as exchange manager was outstanding, but his experiences made him painfully aware that he had little in the way of formal tools. That motivated him to head to Harvard Business School, where valuable additions to his tool kit worked a subtle but significant change in his identity. No longer a kid with zero business experience, he saw himself at graduation as a young executive with years of experience and a set of tools to apply in the business world. The experiences and tools he had acquired reinforced his identity as a manager adept at understanding consumers. Not surprisingly, when he graduated from Harvard Business School, he chose a job in marketing at P&G rather than a competing offer from a strategy consultant.

The feedback loop from experiences to tools happened again during his time as president of P&G's Asia-Pacific region. Based in Japan, he observed how the best Japanese firms typically had an obsessive concern for the design of the consumer experience—from the product itself to its packaging to the experiences of shopping for it in a store. The experience led him to believe that design could be a competitive advantage for P&G. He set out to improve his personal understanding of design by creating the post of vice president of design, establishing an external design advisory board, and developing a close working relationship with IDEO, a leading industrial design firm. As his skills and sensitivities deepened, he became a champion of design in business.

Experiences Can Deepen Mastery

Mastery requires repeated experiences in a particular domain. Because masters in their domain have seen particular phenomena before and know what they mean, they don't have to interpret every sensation or input from scratch as a novice would. In the essentially infinite morass of data, they can pull out the few salient data points that make a difference and mentally map their causal relationships. And because they have done it many times before, they know from experience how to structure the problem in order to create a resolution.

A masterful doctor may be able to diagnose appendicitis after a brief examination of a patient, while a newly minted intern may have to work through dozens of potential options before recognizing what is causing the patient's abdominal pain. The intern might recognize the vague categorical level of "abdominal pain," but the master physician—with her sensitivity to small differences that only experience can teach—recognizes the precise category of "appendicitis-induced pain." From their vast databank of experiences, masters develop pattern-recognition skills that open up shortcuts to solutions.

Mastery isn't gained by accident. It comes only through planned and structured repetition of a consistent type of experience. That is why I argue that experiences don't necessarily deepen mastery. When you've hit one hundred thousand tennis forehands, you have a better chance of hitting a good forehand in the middle of an important match. But to become masterful, the tennis player who hits one hundred thousand forehands needs a plan for carrying out the forehand stroke and a structure for observing and reflecting on the results of each hit. The player who lacks a plan and a structure is likely to develop bad habits and make inconsistent shots.

From his time running the exchange for the Navy, Lafley structured his experiences to continually deepen his mastery. He would hold a sale midweek rather than on the weekend, then "mine the hell out of the data" to see how the sale performed. The learning he acquired from the experience deepened his mastery. At P&G, he continued to deepen his understanding of consumers by repeatedly listening to needs and wants, taking responsive action, and measuring the results against expectations to hone his understanding. Through a conscious campaign of repeated, structured, and planned experiences, Lafley over the course of his career has become a past master of creating, branding, and selling consumer products.

Experiences Can Nurture Originality

Some contexts don't reward the repetition, structuring, and planning that are the hallmarks of mastery. Those nonstandard contexts require the creation of a new approach or solution—that is, originality. Originality demands a willingness to experiment, spontaneity in response to a novel situation, and openness to trying something different than perhaps first planned or intended. Rooted as it is in experiment, originality openly courts failure. It's important to become comfortable with the process of trial and error and iterative prototyping, or you'll be tempted to focus on the less risky mode of mastery, to the exclusion of originality.

Throughout his career, Lafley made a conscious effort to nurture his originality. At the Navy Exchange, he had the spontaneity to seize the opportunity when he got word of the oil price increase. Later he showed openness when he spent endless hours reading the voluntaries from the compact detergent consumer research. The information he gleaned from them helped him engineer a novel response to the consumer research findings. Still later he boldly experimented with the launch of Joy dish liquid in Japan, accepting that he had to engage in a crapshoot to have the chance of accomplishing his goals.

Those experiences showed Lafley that he could successfully take the risks that come with originality. When he took over as CEO in 2000, his confidence in his originality was great enough that he was comfortable making some of the boldest moves in P&G's history, including the Connect & Develop initiative and the Gillette acquisition. His experiences with originality, stretching all the way back to the ceramic elephants, gave him the courage and confidence to take big risks in search of even bigger rewards.

The Most Powerful Experiences:
Mastery Combined with Originality

Mastery and originality need each other to grow. With a wealth of experiences behind him, Lafley can respond quickly when either mastery or originality are called for. In fact, his ability to toggle rapidly between modes sometimes gives others the impression that he has multiple personalities. There's the precise, controlled, expert data-cruncher, working his way methodically through consumer surveys to reach a decision that seems completely data-driven. In the next moment, he can make another decision on what appears to be pure intuition. In fact, as much art as science likely went into the data-driven decision, and as much rigorous analysis as intuition went into the decision that appeared to come straight from the gut. At this stage in his career, most of Lafley's decisions draw on the complementary power of mastery and originality.

Using experiences to drive a combination of mastery and originality is characteristic of integrative thinkers. Moses Znaimer believes that carefully controlling and organizing Citytv's spending is an important part of his job as CEO. It's a skill acquired through years of experience. At the same time, Znaimer has been a pioneer of what he calls "radical broadcasting." The word "visionary" is overused in business, but Znaimer's originality has an element of the visionary to it. "Entrepreneurs like me have a necessary myopia," he says. "We are seized by an idea, compelled, obsessed by it. I don't ask where it all comes from. I just wake up and know what I want to do." Znaimer recognizes the need for the difficult combination of mastery and originality.[3]

Similarly, educator Gerry Mabin shows the ability to manage the tension between mastery and originality in the running of The Mabin School, the innovative institution she founded in Toronto. Her deep expertise in childhood education and learning gave her a strong ability to predict the development of each student based on the school's pedagogical approach. Every element of the school was designed with the express intent of opening a specific learning pathway for her students. At the same time, her pedagogical approach made liberal use of the surprise and spontaneity the students themselves created. In fact, it's fair to say the students' surprises drove the learning process. "You move along with them," Mabin says; "they pull you along."[4]

A famous piece of Mabin School lore concerns a student trip to a museum about ten blocks from the school. The students were all ready to leave for the museum when a flash downpour delayed their departure. When the downpour stopped, the children began walking with their teacher down a steep hill leading to the museum. Halfway there, the children became engrossed by the way the water from the downpour foamed and swirled into the storm sewers along the road. The teacher, rather than insist that the children stick to the plan and march to the museum, created an impromptu lesson on the flowing water. That spontaneous learning experience is now a school legend, and no student who was part of that excursion regrets never making to it to the museum.

As Lafley, Znaimer, and Mabin illustrate, the great ones utilize their experiences to build and deepen their mastery while maintaining and expressing their originality. Average leaders do one or the other. Some deepen their mastery over time but never learn to trust their ability to express originality. They keep the proverbial trains running but will never invent the future. "Watch out," warns Amy Edmondson of the Harvard Business School, "because our natural tendencies, the way we are hardwired, will lead us to favor mastery over originality, will lead us to keep going in the direction we are going and try to improve marginally around the edges on what we're already doing. In so doing, we utterly miss opportunities to make a big difference, something brand new and exciting."[5]

Others express their originality but do not develop their mastery. They are sought out as "idea people" but aren't trusted to run organizations of size and endurance because they can't or won't cultivate the multiple masteries that leadership of such entities demands.

Mastery without originality becomes rote. The master who never tries to think in novel ways keeps seeing the same points of salience, the same causal relationships, and the same problem architecture. Such mastery will produce the same kind of resolution every time, even if the context demands something different. Mastery without originality becomes a cul-de-sac.

By the same token, originality without mastery is flaky if not entirely random. Mastery is required to distinguish between salient and unrelated features, to understand what causal relationships are in play, and how to analyze a complex problem. Without such mastery, the creative resolution is likely to be a random guess. It might succeed once, but there's little chance of repeated and consistent success. Perhaps the most famous example of mastery enabling originality is Pablo Picasso. His cubist revolution may lead those who don't know of his earlier work to think of him as being entirely original, but those familiar with his pre-cubist work know him as master of traditional painting. His mastery enabled him to generate a truly original breakthrough in modern art.

At its core, integrative thinking requires the integration of mastery and originality. Without mastery there won't be a useful salience, causality, or architecture. Without originality, there will be no creative resolution. Without creative resolution, there will be no enhancement of mastery, and when mastery stagnates, so does originality. Mastery is an enabling condition for originality, which in turn, is a generative condition for mastery. The modes are interdependent.

Personal Knowledge as a System

It's hard to overemphasize how much stance, tools, and experience reinforce each other. Each time you use generative reasoning, causal modeling, and assertive inquiry to construct a creative resolution, you deepen your understanding of the tools used to produce the constructive outcome and reinforce the belief that you are capable of forging creative resolutions.

You also improve the odds that your next attempt to fashion a creative resolution will succeed, because you bring a greater level of skill to the task at hand. Success, in turn, will reinforce your optimistic stance and your confidence in your skills. Integrative thinkers continually gain experiences that deepen their mastery and make them more confident they can handle complexity as they approach a creative resolution.

For some, the positive spiral starts young. In the early days of the Institute for OneWorld Health, Victoria Hale got to be known among her colleagues as Dr. Why Not. "People would say

to me, 'Oh that will never work,'" she remembers. "And my response to them would be, 'Why not?'" That's not far at all from
her stance as a child, when she questioned everything she was
taught, preferring to decide for herself what she believed. "Who
says this is the answer?" was a characteristic question of hers.[6]

In due course, she figured out that it was rarely productive to
blurt out her thoughts in that particular form. But though she
grew more tactful, her stance didn't change. Repeated practice in
the creative resolution of tensions reinforced her view that the existing models aren't the only ones, motivated her to acquire tools
that made the job of model creation easier, and honed the sensitivities and skills she needed to find the creative resolutions she
sought.

Repetition also boosted her confidence. She knew that what
she tried to do on a daily basis was difficult; but at the same time,
she knew from long experience that it could be done. She had
used her opposable mind so often that, as Thomas C. Chamberlin
predicted, she developed her thinking pattern as an unconscious
habit.

Hale was by no means alone among the integrative thinkers I
interviewed. Almost to a person, they were confident but not
cocky. They had acquired faith in the deep sensitivities and skills
they had accumulated over years of experience, and with those
skills came a stance infused with calm optimism.

Advancing Experiential Knowledge

None of us can go back to our childhood to practice creating
new models in the face of existing ones. But we can benefit

greatly from experiences going forward. To do so, we need to think about our own thinking as described in chapter 6. Only if we record our predictions in some fashion will we be able to audit the actual outcome against our expectations and learn from our experiences.

A. G. Lafley is highly disciplined about exploring his own thinking. He always wants to know "what would we have to believe" for this conclusion to be robust, just as we learned in chapter 6 to ask what would have to be true for a particular model to be valid.[7]

By asking his question in advance, Lafley creates a logical audit trail for his decision. If the decision doesn't produce the desired outcome, he can review what had to be true for the decision to be a sound one and figure out what he got wrong or what salient data he overlooked. Like Bob Young getting a little better every day, he builds what he learned from experience into his next model, becoming slightly more skilled each time.

To ensure that students and executives at Rotman's integrative thinking courses maximize the learning benefit of their experiences, we teach them to audit and record the logic of their own decisions, and compare the results to the outcomes they predicted. If the results are consistent with their predictions, the validity of their tools and stance is reinforced, building confidence for the next decision cycle. If the results are inconsistent, class participants can ask themselves: what changes in the tools used or the guiding stance could have produced a better outcome? With a relatively small amount of practice, participants can become proficient in reverse engineering their decisions and auditing the results.

The Personal Knowledge System
of the Integrative Thinker

Over the course of this book, we have mapped the typical features of the integrative thinker's personal knowledge system—her stance, tools, and experiences. They are graphically depicted in figure 8-1.

With this combination of stance, tools, and experiences, integrative thinkers grow continually more proficient at generating creative resolutions. This personal knowledge system can help you become more proficient, too. But you will need patience and reflection as you learn.

With respect to patience, to be a truly inspired integrative thinker, you need a wealth of experiences to hone your sensitivities and skills. For most, those sensitivities and skills will take years if not decades to build—"time takes time," as they say in twelve-step groups. By adopting the six attributes of the stance, you can

FIGURE 8-1

Integrative thinker knowledge system

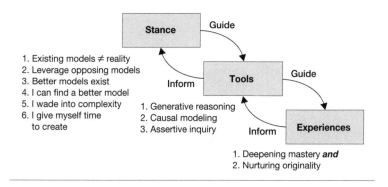

give time a hand, as it were, by creating a structure that will help you develop the tools you will need and direct you toward experiences that build sensitivities and skills.

As for reflection, it speeds you along the path to integrative thinking by maximizing what you learn from each new experience. Our tendency is to think and do rather than think about how we think. The late, great Peter Drucker commented on this point in a speech in 1965:

> *One always finds that the most obvious, the simplest, the clearest conclusion has not been drawn except by a very small fraction of the practitioners. One always finds that the obvious is not seen at all. Perhaps this is simply saying that we never see the obvious as long as we take it for granted.*[8]

In the spirit of Drucker's insight, this book has attempted to chronicle the obvious that has been taken for granted. The obvious is that highly successful managerial leaders think differently than the great mass of their counterparts. The integrative thinking they employ is not rocket science; it is sensible and practical thinking. But such thinking requires the mastery and originality that can only come from experience. Reflection, which defeats the tendency to take the obvious for granted, is what gives experience value. When you refuse to take your thinking for granted, you give yourself the best opportunity to enhance and utilize your opposable mind to its fullest.

Good luck as you build your personal knowledge system, dear reader, and learn the art and science of integrative thinking. Work hard, think hard, and don't dawdle. The world needs you.

Notes

Chapter 1

1. F. Scott Fitzgerald, *The Crack-Up* (New York: New Directions Publishing, 1945).

2. Michael Lee-Chin, in discussion with author at the Rotman School, Toronto, February 28, 2002.

3. *Forbes* 2006 List of Billionaires. Lee-Chin ranked 365 with $2.1 billion net worth, see http://www.forbes.com/lists/2006/10/7TE8.html.

4. All monetary references in the book converted to and denominated in U.S. dollars except those contained within the quotes of a speaker.

5. Andrew Willis, "AIC's Disadvantage: No Street Friends," *Globe and Mail*, September 2, 1999.

6. Thomas C. Chamberlin, "The Method of Multiple Working Hypotheses," *Science* XV, no. 366 (February 7, 1890): 93.

7. Wallace Stevens, "Notes Toward an Extreme Fiction," *The Collected Poems of Wallace Stevens* (New York: Vintage Books, 1990), 380.

8. A. G. Lafley, in discussion with author at the Rotman School, Toronto, November 21, 2005.

9. Bob Young, in discussion with author at the Rotman School, Toronto, September 23 and October 6, 2005.

10. Larry Bossidy and Ram Charan, *Execution: The Discipline of Getting Things Done* (New York: Crown Business, 2002); Jim Collins, *Good to Great: Why Some Companies Make the Leap . . . And Others Don't* (New York: HarperCollins, 2001); Jack Welch, *Jack: Straight from the Gut* (New York: Warner Business, 2001).

11. Bossidy and Charan, *Execution*, 22.

12. Collins, *Good to Great*, 37

13. Chamberlin, *Science*, 94.

Chapter 2

1. A. G. Lafley, in discussion with author at the Rotman School, Toronto, November 21, 2005.

2. Isadore Sharp, in discussion with author at the Rotman School, Toronto, April 11, 2002.

3. Kevin Libin, "Four Seasons Hotels," *Canadian Business*, June 23, 2003, 48.

4. Roger Hallowell, "Four Seasons Hotels and Resorts," Case 9-800-385 (Boston: Harvard Business School, 2000).

5. *Fortune*, "Best Companies to Work For" annual lists, 1998–2006.

6. The concept of an "activity system" is drawn from Michael Porter, "What Is Strategy?" *Harvard Business Review*, November-December 1996, 61–70.

Chapter 3

1. Craig Wynett, in discussion with author at Proctor & Gamble, Cincinnati, Ohio, October 18, 2006.

2. Jordan Peterson, in discussion with author at the Rotman School, Toronto, November 24, 2004.

3. The concepts behind this example draw heavily on a lifetime of work by Chris Argyris, for example as discussed in Chris Argyris, *Overcoming Organizational Defenses* (Boston: Allyn & Bacon, 1990).

4. John Sterman, in discussion with author at the Rotman School, Toronto, March 23, 2003.

5. Jack Neff, "Does P&G Still Matter?" *Advertising Age*, July 25, 2000.

6. A. G. Lafley, in discussion with author at the Rotman School, Toronto, November 21, 2005.

7. See http://www.alumni.hbs.edu/news_events/alumni_achievement /2004_lafley.html.

8. Larry Huston and Nabil Sakkab, "Connect and Develop: Inside Procter & Gamble's New Model for Innovation," *Harvard Business Review*, March 2006, 58–66.

9. Bob Young, in discussion with author at the Rotman School, Toronto, September 23 and October 6, 2003.

10. Piers Handling, in discussion with author at the Rotman School, Toronto, March 7, 2002.

11. Brenda Bouw, "25 Years of Toronto's Film Festival," *The National Post*, May 8, 2000.

12. Liam Lacey, "TIFF/Outpacing Sundance, Passing Cannes," *Globe and Mail*, September 3, 2005.

13. Gina McIntyre, "Buzz Bin," *Hollywood Reporter*, September 6–12, 2005.

14. A. G. Lafley, in discussion with author at the Rotman School, Toronto, November 21, 2005.

Chapter 4

1. See http://www.medaloffreedom.com/MarthaGraham.htm; http://www.time.com/time/time100/artists/profile/graham.html.

2. Subsequent facts concerning Martha Graham from http://www.kennedy-center.org/honors/history/honoree/graham.html; http://www.biography.com/search/article.do?id=9317723.

3. Daniel Levinthal and James March, "The Myopia of Learning," *Strategic Management Journal*, 14 (Special Issue, Winter 1993): 95–112.

4. Peter Drucker, in discussion with author at the Rotman School, Toronto, June 12, 2002.

5. Hilary Austen, in discussion with author at the Rotman School, Toronto, March 25, 2002.

6. F. C. Kohli, in discussion with author at the Rotman School, Toronto, October 5, 2006.

7. Bruce Mau, in discussion with author at the Rotman School, Toronto, November 2, 2004.

8. Tim Brown, in discussion with author at the Rotman School, Toronto, January 15, 2004.

9. Moses Znaimer, in discussion with author at the Rotman School, Toronto, April 10, 2002.

Chapter 5

1. I am indebted to Hilary Austen Johnson for the thinking behind the stance, tools, and experiences framework. I became familiar with her thinking on personal knowledge systems during the writing of her dissertation at Stanford University; this chapter has strong roots in that work. For those wanting to read more of her work, see Hilary Austen Johnson, "Artistry for the Strategist," *Journal of Business Strategy*, vol. 28, issue 4 (2007): 13–21.

2. Bob Young, in discussion with author at the Rotman School, Toronto, September 23, October 6, 7, 27, and 28, December 1 and 2, 2003.

3. Marshall McCluhan, *Understanding Media: The Extensions of Man* (New York: McGraw-Hill, 1964; republished by Gingko Press, 2003).

4. Sumantra Ghoshal, "Bad Management Theories Are Destroying Good Management Practices," *Academy of Management Learning and Education* 4, no. 1 (2005): 75–91.

5. Richard Nelson and Sidney Winter, *An Evolutionary Theory of Economic Change* (Cambridge: Harvard University Press, 1982).

Chapter 6

1. Victoria Hale, in discussion with author in San Francisco, December 15, 2006.

2. See http://www.macfound.org/site/c.lkLXJ8MQKrH/b.959463/k.9D7D/Fellows_Program.htm.

3. Meg Whitman, in discussion at the Rotman School conference, Toronto, January 28, 2005.

4. Nandan Nilekani, in discussion with author at the Rotman School, Toronto, September, 16, 2002.

5. Jack Welch, in discussion with author at the Rotman School, Toronto, September 12, 2005.

6. Ramalinga Raju, in discussion with author at the Rotman School, Toronto, October 26, 2004.

7. Bruce Mau, in discussion with author at the Rotman School, Toronto, November 2, 2004.

8. The derivation of contented model defense is from the original work of Karl Popper on justificationism in Karl Popper, *The Logic of Scientific Discovery* (London: Hutchinson, 1959).

9. Nathan Houser and Christian Kloesel, eds., *The Essential Peirce: Selected Philosophical Writings (1867–1893)*, vol. 1 (Bloomington: Indiana University Press, 1992), and Peirce Edition Project, eds., *The Essential Peirce: Selected Philosophical Writings (1893–1913)*, vol. 2 (Bloomington: Indiana University Press, 1998). Later, Karl Popper developed the concept of falsificationism (also in *The Logic of Scientific Discovery* cited above). While apparently it was not based on Peirce's work because Popper only came upon it later, it reinforces and builds on Peirce's fallibilism. Later still, Imre Lakatos built further with the concept of sophisticated methodological falsificationism; see Imre Lakatos, "Falsification and the Logic of Scientific Research Programmes," in Imre Lakatos and Alan Musgrave, *Criticism and the Growth of Knowledge* (New York: Cambridge University Press, 1970). My optimistic model seeker construct is meant to combine the concepts of Peirce's fallibilism and Lakatos' sophisticated methodological falsificationism.

10. Bob Young, in discussion with author at the Rotman School, Toronto, September 23 and October 6, 2003.

11. Michael Lee-Chin, in discussion with author at the Rotman School, Toronto, February 28, 2001.

12. K. V. Kamath, in discussion with author at the Rotman School, Toronto, April 16, 2004.

13. Robert McEwen, in discussion with author at the Rotman School, Toronto, October 18, 2006.

14. Jan Rivkin, "Imitation of Complex Strategies," *Management Science* 46, no. 6 (June 2000): 824–844; and Mihnea Moldoveanu and Robert Bauer, "On the Relationship Between Organizational Complexity and Organizational Structuration," *Organization Science* 15, no. 1 (January 2004): 98–118.

Chapter 7

1. Taddy Blecher, in discussion with author at the Rotman School, Toronto, September 16, 2006.

2. Education in South Africa, see http://www.southafrica.info/ess _info/sa_glance/education/education.htm.

3. David White, "How to Build a University at Minimum Cost," *Financial Times*, June 6, 2006.

4. Peirce, *The Essential Peirce* (vols. 1 and 2).

5. James March, Lee Sproull, and Michal Tamuz, "Learning from Samples of One or Fewer," *Organization Science* 2 (1991): 1–13.

6. John Sterman, in discussion with author at the Rotman School, Toronto, March 24, 2003.

7. Jay Forrester, *Industrial Dynamics* (Cambridge: Pegasus Press, 1961).

8. George Lakoff and Mark Johnson, *Philosophy in the Flesh: The Embodied Mind and Challenge to Western Philosophy* (New York: Basic Books, 1999).

9. His body of work includes books in which he describes this technique including: Chris Argyris, *Knowledge for Action* (San Francisco: Jossey-Bass, 1993).

Chapter 8

1. A. G. Lafley, in discussion with author at the Rotman School, Toronto, November 21, 2005.

2. Procter & Gamble 2006 Annual Report, note 2, p. 49.

3. Moses Znaimer, in discussion with author at the Rotman School, Toronto, April 10, 2002.

4. Gerry Mabin, in discussions with author at the Rotman School, Toronto, February 16, 2001.

5. Amy Edmondson, in discussion with author at the Rotman School, Toronto, October 24, 2004.

6. Victoria Hale, in discussion with author in San Francisco, December 15, 2006.

7. A. G. Lafley, in discussion with author at the Rotman School, Toronto, November 21, 2005.

8. Peter Drucker, "Entrepreneurship in Business Enterprise," speech presented at the University of Toronto, March 3, 1965; "Commercial Letter" (Head Office, Toronto: Canadian Imperial Bank of Commerce, March 1965, 11–12).

Index

About the Author

Roger Martin has served since 1998 as Dean of the Joseph L. Rotman School of Management, University of Toronto, where he holds the Premier's Research Chair in Competitiveness and Productivity. At Rotman, he also chairs the AIC Centre for Corporate Citizenship, the Desautels Centre for Integrative Thinking, the Collaborative for Health Sector Strategy, and the Institute for Competitiveness and Prosperity.

Martin holds an AB from Harvard University (1979) and an MBA from Harvard Business School (1981). He was a member of the group of HBS classmates who grew Monitor Company from a tiny start-up to one of the world's leading strategy consulting firms, and served as co-head of the firm in 1995 and 1996. He continues to serve as an adviser to CEOs of large global companies.

His previous book, *The Responsibility Virus* (Basic Books), was published in 2002. Martin writes extensively for publications such as the *Harvard Business Review*, the *Financial Times*, *Fast Company*, and *Barron's* and is a regular online columnist for *BusinessWeek*.

In 2004, Martin was awarded the Marshal McLuhan Award for Visionary Leadership. In 2005, he was named one of *BusinessWeek*'s seven "Innovation Gurus." In 2007, he was named a *BusinessWeek*

"B-School All-Star" for being one of the ten most influential business professors in the world, based on the integrative thinking work that is the subject of this book.

Martin serves on the boards of Thomson Corporation, Research in Motion, the Skoll Foundation, the Canadian Credit Management Foundation, and Tennis Canada and is a Trustee of the Hospital for Sick Children. He is Chairman of the Ontario Task Force on Competitiveness, Productivity and Economic Progress.